The Alchemy
of
True Success

Activate Your Mind
◆
Revitalize Your Body
◆
Reignite Your Spirit

JADEN STERLING

WEALTH OF WISDOM
PUBLISHING

Wealth of Wisdom Publishing
200 Second Avenue S.
Suite 203
St. Petersburg, FL 33701

The information presented herein represents the views of the author as of the date of publication. This book is presented for informational purposes only. Due to the rate at which conditions change, the author reserves the right to alter and update his opinions at any time. While every attempt has been made to verify the information in this book, the author does not assume any responsibility for errors, inaccuracies, or omissions.

Cover Design by Anna Modig

ISBN 978-0988816312 (Wealth of Wisdom Publishing)
ISBN 0988816318
Self-Development/Success

Contents

Preface i

Introduction iv

Part I – Activate Your Instrument of Change: *Mind*

Chapter 1:   Discover Your Inner Alchemist......................... 1

Chapter 2:   How I Succeeded—And You Can Too 9

Chapter 3:   Go Within So You Won't Go Without............ 19

Chapter 4:   Let Go...27

Chapter 5:   Overcome the Blame Game..........................45

Chapter 6:   How Conscious Are You? 55

Chapter 7:   Be Present in the Moment 65

Chapter 8:   Reconnect Through the Inner Voyage.............. 79

Chapter 9:   Harness the Power of Your Mind 93

Chapter 10: Setting Intentions Gets the Universe's Attention. 105

Part II – Revitalize Your Vessel: *Body*

Chapter 11: How to Activate Your Magnetic Center:
             Your Brain's Core.. 129

Chapter 12: Improving Your Health Benefits More Than
             Your Body 145

Part III – Reignite Your Fire: *Spirit*

Chapter 13: Ignite Your Spirit.. 181

Chapter 14: The Golden Grid: How to Manifest Anything 203

Chapter 15: Take Risks – Your Success Depends On It!...217

Conclusion 237

Acknowledgments 241

About the Author 245

Preface

For over 25 years I've delved into nearly all aspects of human potential and personal development, especially as it relates to success. During those years, one single question stayed in the forefront of my mind: *How do we manifest a life of our choosing?*

Intuitively, I've always known we have much more control over our life than we are led to believe. I've also known that life doesn't just happen to us. Truth is we are the creators of our experiences. In an effort to answer this simple question: *how do we create our experiences*? I was led to study the ancient art of alchemy.

Alchemists centuries ago were able to transform lesser base metals into gold. Alchemists mastered the art of transmutation by applying their knowledge (which often came to them through deep meditation) to physical objects, transforming them and increasing their value. Upon discovering this, I knew I had figured out *how* and *why* we are able to transmute our desires into physical reality.

This is the very reason that I wrote this book. I wanted to share this amazing information with you so that you too can manifest the life of your dreams. After all, I see too many people in developed countries suffering needlessly when it comes to their finances, health, and overall wellbeing. A large percentage of the population is experiencing financial stress and they don't have to.

Throughout history, we've observed people, societies, and cultures thriving, suffering or just getting by, regardless of their economic environment. So, what sets them apart? What are the distinguishing characteristics of those who thrive and those who don't?

You might be as surprised as I was when I found out the answers to those questions.

The Alchemy of True Success is one of those rare books that can change your life in the course of a couple of nights' reading. However, please don't misunderstand this book's message and dismiss it as being too simple to be effective. You will find throughout the pages of this book, that true success is about following your heart, not your head. About letting go, rather than grasping. About trusting your instincts and your gut feelings. It's about the alchemy of success and your ability to effectively use your God-given toolset: mind, body and spirit.

A lot of the information in this book came when I began tapping into my own mind, body and spirit connection. Many nights I was awakened by my helpers in the spiritual realm with ideas and concepts for this book. The process for me is a regular occurrence now but several years ago it was a strange feeling. I soon learned I had a team of "spiritual professionals" comprised of ascended masters: spirit guides, Archangels, and yes, the energy most refer to as God. This team comes to me as The One Voice and assists me in sharing information with you through a process called channeled writing. The process is simple: I sit in a quiet location, focus my thoughts on what messages people need to hear, and then I wait to receive guidance. Soon after, I feel and hear spoken words that I then write down or record on my phone and have transcribed later.

I am never concerned with attracting negativity or beings of lower vibration to me during this process. Because of my knowing that only good comes to me, I experience beautiful white light energy around me during these channeling sessions. So, there you have it. I said it. Yes, I communicate with non-physical beings who always give amazing insight and guidance, which makes my life simple, easy and graceful. The majority of the information, ideas and concepts in this book were either given to me directly from The One Voice or are based on my own experiences, which I'm excited to share with you.

You might be wondering at this point if you, too, can tap into the amazing guidance available from the spiritual realm. My answer is a resounding "yes!". Come on this journey with me, and I'll show you how.

Introduction

The Alchemy of True Success is not your typical book on material success. Multi-dimensional and heart-centered, this book is built on the premise that we are spiritual beings living from the heart and desiring financial abundance and soul fulfillment.

I believe there's a huge difference between achieving success versus achieving *true* success.

In the title of this book I put the word "true" in front of the word "success" because at your very core, you are in fact a truth seeker. Being a truth seeker means you are naturally inquisitive about the ways and workings of the universe. And you desire to fulfill your soul's purpose during your short stint on Earth. The journey of the truth seeker is for those who are brave at heart, who are willing to blaze their own trail, and are willing to turn inward, asking and answering some deep questions. I know this to be true since I am a truth seeker as well, and have helped people just like you define for themselves what it takes to live a life of true success. In this book, I give you the steps with simple and clear directives to follow for you to achieve a life of true success. If you're envisioning yourself living a balanced life filled with purpose and passion yet need help getting there, you're in the right place. The answers are here.

The *Alchemy of True Success* shares how to use the tools you already have—your mind, body and spirit—to transform your inner dreams and goals so that they become your reality. This book takes you on a journey to self, awakening you to the magnificence that is your natural state of being and reminding you of your deep spiritual connection to your true essence and to all that is.

Rather than the end result, the experience you choose for yourself is the most important thing to consider as it relates to true success. The rules of engagement are the same for experiencing both success and true success, which is to offer a product or service that people need or want. True success, however, is found in one's ability to look beyond personal wants and contribute to the needs of others, society, and the planet. In doing so, your life (and your soul) will be more fulfilled than you ever imagined. If your objective is only to make lots of money or have the ability to purchase countless material objects, then true success will surely elude you.

As evidenced by its ability to ebb and flow in your life, money is transmutable and liquid. However, something even more valuable exists beyond what money can buy, and that is soul fulfillment. Fulfillment comes from pursuing one's purpose and passion. Being of service to others is a necessary component of true success and feeds one's soul beyond the toys that money can buy. Now, please hear me, I don't recommend that you shun money or follow a path of austerity. Rather, I suggest a balanced approach as it relates to the spiritual and financial aspects that already exist inside of you.

Furthermore, I believe each person holds the answers within to determine what's right for them. Everyone is here on Earth for reasons far greater than just making money and pursuing "the American dream." In the big scheme of things, your life is short, so isn't it worth taking the time to start asking and answering some very deep questions for yourself?

The Ancient Secrets of Alchemy

I believe that the law of attraction and the principles of manifesting have roots based in the centuries-old practice of alchemy. These practices, which are based upon truths gleaned from ancient alchemists, have become an essential component of growth in our present times.

This book is designed to explore those sacred truths. Your mind, your body and your spirit can take you further than you have ever dreamed. Within this book, you will discover what it takes to have a plentiful life composed of true success. It's a life that is balanced, fulfilling, joyful and abundant.

The rewarding journey to achieving your desires isn't mysterious or arduous; in fact, the steps are simple. The greatest challenge you face is reforming your thought processes and becoming open to the changes that are possible. You'll learn how to eliminate restrictive thinking and to trust in the immense power that exists within and around you.

Humans hold this potential within themselves, but many have forgotten this truth due to psychic amnesia. Before your spirit came into your physical body to pass another lifetime on Earth, an angel touched your upper lip with their index finger and gently whispered, "Don't remember."

The aim of this project is a collective remembrance of that which makes us divine, a recollection of the connection that we have to the universe.

The world in which we live is complex and at times can feel overwhelming as we go about our days. The planet is filled to overflowing with the energy and lives of more than seven billion people, all of whom are consumed by their own personal journeys. Each person has physical characteristics that set him or her apart from everyone else. Even identical twins have unique fingerprints, eye prints and other physical qualities that make them unique. In addition to the unique physical qualities that humans possess, every person experiences a unique existence as a result of their beliefs, thoughts, feelings and emotions.

For every person who has the sincere desire to achieve true success, there exists a way forward. There exists a special solution for you and you alone. The solution holds the answers to your deepest questions. As your guide, I wish to lead you into the discovery of the place where your loftiest dreams are born – and from there assist you in creating a life worth living. A life that is fulfilling and purposeful. A life that acknowledges and answers the deep questions of your soul.

You were brought to this book for a reason. Trust that, and may you have an open mind and a willing heart to turn the page and begin your journey.

✸ SELF-ASSESSMENTS

Throughout *The Alchemy of True Success* you'll see sections titled "Self-Assessments." These are designed to maximize your growth. For the best results, you may want to use a journal in which to make notes and answer the questions. The more time you invest in answering the questions, the more you'll learn about yourself and the more growth you'll experience.

Part I

Activate Your
Instrument of Change:
Mind

Chapter 1:
Discover Your Inner Alchemist

"You are an alchemist; make gold of that."
~ William Shakespeare

Every individual is an alchemist. You are an alchemist, and this book is built upon this premise.

You might be reading this and thinking, "What the heck is alchemy?"

The subject of alchemy isn't one that you encounter in most day-to-day conversations. Few people are talking about the most recent sorcerer who happened into town and began changing base substances into gold. In fact, for most people the term "sorcerer" brings to mind the pointy-hatted character in the "Sorcerer's Apprentice" segment of Disney's *Fantasia*. Be that as it may, there was a time in history when enlightened sorcerers truly did possess the knowledge of how to transform metal into gold.

The origins of alchemy can be traced to several different ancient cultures, including China, Egypt, and India, each of which devised their own separate theories and beliefs. Owing to the lack of communication, each retained their own separate secrets until travel increased and trade routes were developed. Amazingly, the concepts were often parallel with one another. The basic tenet was that lower metals could be transmuted into gold, which was considered the perfect and most valuable metal.

The ability to perform this transmutation was limited to a select few. These worthy alchemists had received access to higher truth through mentorship with master teachers and deep meditation. Alchemists held to the simple yet significant rule that's still essential to the universal practice: *One instrument, one vessel and one fire.* For this reason, I arranged this book in such a way to reflect the tools of the alchemists as they relate to the tools you already possess. These tools are: One instrument (your mind), one vessel (your body), and one fire (your spirit). After reading this book you will know how to properly use each. If you follow the steps and do the self-assessments your life could very well be transformed so much you might even feel as if you struck gold!

In the alchemists search for self-knowing, they communed with and studied the aspects of the soul agent. The conduit of being that they discovered took the form of a serpentine power that moves upward in spirals. This powerful symbol is also often referred to as *kundalini* or life-force energy.

> *KUNDALINI – (Sanskrit kund, "to burn"; kunda, "to coil or to spiral") a concentrated field of intelligent, cosmic invisible energy absolutely vital to life; beginning in the base of the spine when a man or woman begins to evolve as wisdom is earned. Kundalini has been described as liquid fire and liquid light. The ultimate outcome of kundalini is the union of Will (sakti-kundalini), Knowledge (prana-kundalini) and Action (para- kundalini).*

Alchemy in Europe

In some cultures the practice degenerated into superstition, but in Egypt it survived as a scholarly discipline. The knowledge traveled to Europe when twelfth-century scholars translated Arabic works into Latin. By the end of the thirteenth century alchemy was discussed seriously by leading philosophers, scientists, and theologians, which eventually led to chemistry as we know it today.

Meanwhile however, practicing alchemists in personal possession of higher knowledge journeyed across Europe, often in secret. Royalty and governments feared such power could disrupt nations, which placed the life of a true alchemist in constant danger. Their sacred mission was to impart their knowledge to those conscious individuals who were able to understand and apply the knowledge.

Alchemists were acquainted with the power of integrating the divine and the human, and they relied heavily upon their deepest dreams, inspirations and visions for guidance in perfecting their art. The sacrosanct knowledge they imparted across the continent truly empowered others and gave them the ability to change all forms of matter. The alchemists used a worthy method from which we can draw inspiration today: first mastering their art and then having the expertise and passion to share it with others.

Over the centuries, the wisdom and value that sprang from this great knowledge inspired people to become conscious practitioners in their own lives. Alchemists understood that a seed of gold, whether taking the shape of a truthful word spoken at the right moment or an actual physical object to be held in the hand, could evoke results a thousand times stronger than knowledge gained from science.

This is why I stated that you are an alchemist. You are a modern-day alchemist who is able to transform aspects of your life by aligning with your true essence. The act of allowing this transformation to take place within you is an infinite gift that holds the power for positive change beyond measure. This same ability—this same enlightenment—lies dormant within the soul of each person in today's world.

Rather than transforming base metal into gold, each person has the ability to transmute his or her dreams into reality.

You may be wondering if there truly is a special solution that belonged to you and you alone, then why do the answers at times seem vague and unattainable? One of the reasons has to do with the distractions that each person faces every day. Our fast-paced, overly stimulated, technologically advanced society is filled with voices, noises, images, and streams of information that come to us through texts, emails, phone calls, and computer programs. All of this stimulation competes for our attention. Added to this are the day-to-day challenges of life that keep us ever tense, stressed, frustrated, and distracted. It's little wonder that solitude, introspection, and total relaxation are hardly even considered in the course of a day.

Those running the rat race to make it through the day, or who are barely able to make ends meet, are usually those operating from a belief system that was formed during their growing-up years. Concepts of success were learned from such sources as parents, guardians, coaches, teachers, professors, peers and guidance counselors.

The advice that most of us received as children and adolescents was extremely limited in scope and context: go to school, get good grades, get a college education, and get a good job. That's it. Now you're set for life.

This advice came because it's what they did and it seemed to work for them, and probably worked for their parents too. More than likely, your parents grew up hearing stories of severe lack and shortages that came by living through the Great Depression.

Sit around any holiday dinner table where the family elders are present, and you'll hear tales of scarcity and how they were able to make do in the worst of times. It's only human nature to want to relive experiences and tell stories from the past.

While you may have heard these stories repeatedly, it's important that you learn to distance yourself from the *fear* that comes with the telling. The fact is that much advice you received in the past may have sprung up out of that basic fear of scarcity.

Your family members had your best interest at heart when they counseled you to play it safe rather than blaze your own trail. Such advice came from a place of love; however, love when shrouded in fear has the power to squelch dreams and goals.

I can't help but wonder how many of our elders harbored a secret yearning deep inside to experience something more in life. The odds are good that a large majority experienced that yearning, but lacked the know-how to go about changing their world.

Perhaps you were told, either in words or by example, that success comes from outside of you via a good job, loving family, large home, expensive cars, plenty of money, and perhaps a little status thrown in for good measure.

The fact that you are reading this book tells me that you're not satisfied with those answers. You're not satisfied with those concepts. You're an independent thinker. You're convinced you can never live a life of freedom playing by someone else's rules. If that's the case, we have work to do.

But don't let the word "work" frighten you away. The work I'm referring to is designed to reawaken your senses and delight your soul. Your journey will lead you back toward the self that always felt safe, confident, joyful and complete. This refers to your authentic self, the very essence of you that lingers inside below the layers of fear or doubt.

Many people have not been in touch with their authentic self since childhood. Children can serve as a wonderful reminder of the joy that comes from being fully present and indulging one's deepest dreams. Children raised in a healthy environment naturally believe that they can be, can do, and can have anything their heart desires without fear or worry.

What Do You Want to Be?

> *"Adults ask children what they want to be when they grow up because they are looking for ideas."*
> ~ Paula Poundstone

The dreams of children are limitless. If you ask children to rank themselves on a scale of one to ten, nearly all will say they're a ten. Children know how to experience life with an excitement that has no bounds.

Even though you're now an adult, it's possible to vividly remember and tap into that excitement. Reach back and bring up those spectacular dreams that were large enough to fill an entire lifetime with joy and success.

My hope for you as you begin this journey is that you'll come face to face with your inner potential, that you'll get in touch with your unique and amazing qualities, and that you'll become aware that you're *still a ten*.

As you read through these chapters you'll quickly learn that in this very moment of time, you possess everything you'll ever need to live a full life of complete and pure success!

Are you ready to start on your journey of true success? Let's get started, shall we?

❋ SELF-ASSESSMENT

◆ Take a moment and think back to when you were a child. What do you remember about your childhood dreams?

◆ As a child, when asked what you wanted to be when you grew up, what did you reply? Can you remember how it felt to believe in your dream without worry or fear?

Log these answers in your journal.

Chapter 2:
How I Succeeded—And
You Can Too

*"Try not to become a man of success, but rather try
to become a man of value."* ~ Albert Einstein

What defines true success? It's a question that we ask ourselves over and over as we pass through the days that compose our lives, always searching for completeness. What drives us in life to succeed, and how do we define our own personal version of prosperity and abundance?

For as long as I can remember, I've been fascinated with stories of success. More specifically, I've been drawn to understand the lives and motivations of successful people themselves, rather than feeling focused on the riches that they've attained. My interest in a life of true success goes much deeper than the ability to acquire possessions or wield power with money. Instead, I've always felt consumed by the desire to understand the ways that successful people treat others, how they live their lives, what dominates their thoughts, what has inspired them to greatness, and whether or not they believe there's more to life than what they experience via their five senses. I've always had the inclination that success comes from within and that it's a force projected out into the world via the spirit. Which brings me to the question, "Can a person or business be successful if they are not in touch with their own being, or soul?" The answer is yes and we see it everyday in businesses that focus on the bottom line, rather than make its front line (employees) and its top line (customers) a priority. However, that is not what this book is about; this book is about the journey every person or business will take in order to experience *true* success.

It has been essential for me to look back and evaluate my own path to success and wholeness. My sojourn toward prosperity began at the age of twelve, when I first read *The Seeds of Greatness* by Denis Waitley. It was my first experience with reading a text that guided me in the direction of building a positive attitude by uniting spirituality with aspiration. The book opened my mind to the endless possibilities that life could have in store for my own unique dreams. The author's message resonated deep within my soul, and I knew that I had discovered basic and essential understandings that would be vital to my success. I began to weave a tapestry of greatness and forward thinking into my plan for my own life. Even though this book was eye opening for me in so many ways, it only laid the groundwork for what was still to come.

I kept the principles that I had learned from this important text in my mind and looked out for other guiding messages from which I could benefit along the way. A few years later another turning point came across my path that had a lasting impact on me. I was invited to hear Zig Ziglar give a talk. It was on the night of my eighteenth birthday, and I jumped at the chance to have this firsthand encounter. You may find it hard to believe, but its true—rather than passing a night in celebration with my friends I chose to spend my birthday listening to Zig Ziglar, who astounded the audience with his stories of success and greatness. I was drawn to understand more information that could assist me along my path, and the night proved to be the best possible birthday present that anyone could have offered! I was in awe as Ziglar confidently delivered his enlightening and entertaining speech to the enraptured crowd, who absorbed his words and hoped to use his knowledge in order to enhance their own lives. My eyes were glued to his every gesture; and when, on bended knee, he promised the audience we could have anything our heart desired, well, I admit I certainly believed him!

Reading Waitley's book and hearing Ziglar speak both helped me to understand that I had all the tools within me to begin my journey toward genuine success. All I needed was the vehicle to help me get there. I realized from both that true success is a *whole-being experience*. You must be in touch with who you are, not just with how much money you've made. If the spirit is acting with intention, the monetary success of life can surely follow; but if the soul is not in touch with our actions, there can be no rewards.

As I began to embark upon a new career in the business world—a young man full of ambition and confidence—I vowed that I would keep these principles in mind.

My twenties were spent working as a consultant for the largest financial-services firm in the world. I followed the words that had guided me in my youth and applied the inspiring messages to my own personal agenda, and in time I did achieve a great deal of success. The money flowed into my hands like water and, not surprisingly, I cheerfully stepped into the role of a voracious consumer. I bought expensive sports cars, purchased an extravagant house on the water, ordered custom-made furniture, and splurged regularly on European vacations. I was gaining just what I thought I had always wanted. I could quantify my life through my earnings, and I could attain nearly any worldly object that I desired.

My days were busy and filled with activities and adventures that I had imagined would fill the hole that I felt inside.

Yet something was missing from my life that I could not put my finger on. I had not kept my spirit in mind as my ambitions had soared up to the mountaintops, and though the view from the top was indeed impressive, I felt empty and alone from where I stood. Looking back upon that time from where I stand today, I can clearly determine that I was out of touch with my original dreams. My wallet was full, but my soul was empty. I found myself looking to others for validation, hoping that, through their admiration, I would be able to experience self-knowing and self-love. I was too busy to step back and examine what was missing and what I needed to do to change my life.

Like so many others have been before me, I was caught up in the trappings of success. I had been seduced into abandoning my earlier definition of true success and greatness, which was to live a joyful, purposeful, peaceful and free life. In my quest for financial gain and higher status in the business world, I had forgotten that the tools I required to live a successful and fulfilling life were all inside me, rather than scattered along the ascent of the corporate ladder. Holding myself back, and hiding behind my business suit, I had somehow *descended* into feeling afraid and unprepared to step into my true life's calling.

Intuitively I knew my life had a deeper purpose in store. I still felt a stirring deep within my heart and soul, a yearning to break away from the chains of consumerism, of pleasure seeking, and experience the ecstasy of true freedom. But how could I make the transition?

My responsibilities as a financial consultant included selecting investments for my clients to help them meet their financial goals. All of my assignments were straightforward and mathematical—operations that required expertise but could be performed almost by rote. I yearned for a creative outlet. Deep down I had a feeling that there must be more to life than what meets the eye, and I began more seriously contemplate some of the principles that I had learned from the mentors whom I had encountered in my youth. I felt there was more to each human than just a physical body, and I even suspected forces greater than myself were at work assisting me along my path.

Have you ever been struck by the deep-seated understanding that the thing you needed to help you through a challenge had come across your path at just the right time? Perhaps you weren't even sure of why or how that force had entered into your life. If you have felt the power of just such a crucial moment, then I'm sure you can relate to the impact that this realization held for me.

As I became more conscious and aware that there were unseen forces greater than myself perpetually aiding me, I began to identify clues and patterns in my daily life that were emerging, and I felt my intuition waking up to messages from the universe. Conversations I had with people around me were incredibly stimulating and helped me realize that I was not alone in experiencing the powerful force of change presenting itself in my life. People all around me were feeling shifts in themselves toward healing and revitalizing energy, their focus shifting away from money and consumerism. They discussed how they were ready to embrace a deeper understanding of their lifelong purpose here on Earth.

Inspired by my revelations, I took a bold step. At the young age of 31, I made a leap of faith and retired from corporate America. I decided to set out upon a journey to discover myself and locate my inner purpose. I knew I wanted to make a positive difference in other people's lives at a deep level—not just helping them to manage their financial accounts, but to help them align their mind, body and spirit in order to guide them in fulfilling their deeper purpose. I felt fresh in my pursuit of self-knowing and began to understand things about my heart and desires that filled the empty hole that I felt inside.

I was led to the work of the ancient alchemists and to examine their understanding of matter as transmutable. In the same spirit, I began to transform my own life into something completely different.

When I allowed myself to dig deeper into what it meant to live a purposeful and fulfilling life, my intuition grew stronger, which naturally led me in the direction of contributing to the growth and positive change that I could see was possible in so many others. The most amazing thing that came from my choice to help others (something I never could have predicted in my wildest dreams), was that contributing to others allowed me to become even more prosperous.

Therein lies a key to true success:
**Take the focus off yourself
and be of service to others.**

Some may believe that taking the focus off themselves and putting it on others won't help them achieve their goals. The concept even sounds (dare I say) counterintuitive. However, the gifts of healing and growth that we receive from being of service to others can never be fabricated by other means. When you reach out to others and extend yourself to them, prosperity will blossom. It's the truth, as you'll see in practice witnessing the genuine benefits that come from helping others!

I thought back to the many conversations I had experienced with peers and colleagues who were facing the same challenges. So many of them had felt a similar magnetism to an energetic shift in their lives, but were unable to make a brave new leap as I had. I decided to share the positive elements that had impacted my life and had allowed my spirit to grow. I began offering personal coaching services to others who might benefit from my journey and helped to guide them along their own.

Assisting others to grow and giving outside of myself have been the greatest gifts of all. I have been able to see others thrive and benefit in their own ways and achieve spectacular goals along their individual paths. The things I've learned from the stories I've encountered in my coaching work would take a lifetime to relate, but I've attempted to capture in this book the basic tenet of the influences that have helped my soul, and theirs, to evolve so that we can experience true success.

My career as a guide along the path to true success has not been linear, but it has been beautiful, and my life is full of amazing gifts that I am ever grateful for. It was only when I looked at the bigger picture that I began to understand what true success means to me, and what it means in one form or another for all humans. When I began to listen to my soul, my intuitive needs, and the voice of the universe, my path to happiness and satisfaction became illuminated.

By sharing my own journey, it's my hope that something in it will resonate with you. However, your definition of true success will be uniquely yours, and revisiting your own vision of success is a great place to begin your journey.

✳ SELF-ASSESSMENT

- ♦ What is your current definition of success?

- ♦ Does your current definition of success include contributing to the wellbeing of others?

- ♦ Do you allow for feelings of gratitude, joy, harmony, peace, grace and love to be a part of your experience when it comes to success?

Chapter 3:
Go Within So You Won't
Go Without

*"Trying to be happy by accumulating possessions is
like trying to satisfy hunger by taping sandwiches all
over your body."* ~ George Carlin

Time and time again, you may find yourself stuck in a
familiar situation. Perhaps you're an employee, trapped within
the confines of the grueling nine-to-five job, living on a tight
budget from paycheck to paycheck, assisting your employer as
they fulfill their dreams. Or maybe you own a business, but you
lack freedom, and find yourself overworked without reaping the
benefits of your labor. The promise of fulfilling your dreams
"someday" gets pushed to the far recesses of your mind, and
making a living takes precedence over developing a high-quality
and satisfying life.

Success is thought of as being one-dimensional, and money
is on a pedestal as the grand prize. Priorities shift from personal
fulfillment to generating a substantial income. And what's the
use of having large sums of money unless you spend it? So

shopping becomes the activity of choice, and soon the trappings of monetary success clutter your house, mind and soul. Worldly gain overpowers spiritual pursuit, creating a self-imposed trap of obligation and materiality. The desire to acquire wealth and show off that wealth with objects will fill one's days, but it will certainly not fill one's soul. Disillusioned with the "American Dream" and deeply entrenched in the financial burden of pursuing it, gratifying one's ego can easily take precedence over soul nurturing. It's an easy cycle to become established in, especially considering that most of the people around you will be digging the same hole.

The emotional pain that comes from being financially burdened and soulfully trapped creates a stirring deep within. Is this a symptom of indigestion that can be easily cured? Hardly! The nature of the problem is deep, and must be dealt with at the root. So many of us experience the familiar pang that resounds within our soul as we struggle with our own dissatisfaction, whether or not we have been able to achieve our goals. The crying out from inside that occurs prompts the weighty question to rise to the surface: *Is this as good as it gets?*

> *True success is measured by what you contribute to others, not by the things you have.*

It's only when you step back from the pursuit of riches, engaging in moments of clarity that can bring about peace and quiet, that the truth you've been seeking can emerge from within.

Contributing to the greater good and living a life of freedom encapsulates the meaning of true success. And contributing without expectation or desiring to gratify one's ego is the basis for which true success is built. And here's the good news: you already have everything you need to move forward into living a life of true success. The instruments of change that you possess are just waiting to be activated.

This is because you're an alchemist. Perhaps not of the ancient variety, who wears robes and experiments with chemical compounds. You're a modern-day alchemist, wielding the most sophisticated and advanced tools that can transform your life; however, I suspect you may not even know it!

The Advanced Tools You Already Possess

"Advanced tools?" you ask. "What are you talking about?"

The advanced tools I refer to are your mind, your body and your spirit. Does it sound like too simple of a solution to actually be real? You may be wondering why they do not already possess success in their lives, given that these so-called tools are already in their grasp. But the mastery of these tools has a steady learning curve, just like any other skill. It's a matter of knowledge rather than educational background, and it's through focused practice that these tools can become an intrinsic part of your successful life.

As with anything, one must select the appropriate tool for a particular task.

For example, if you had a large and unsightly dead tree in your yard, you might wish to remove it. Would your first thought be to seek out something sharp with which to cut it down, perhaps a knife from the kitchen drawer? Logical reasoning tells us that knives are sharp and can cut things, but is this really the best tool for the job? The answer is, of course, no. The situation will have a more effective outcome if you use a proper tool such as a chain saw. That example may sound silly to some, yet how many people each day reach for the wrong tools, hoping in vain that this action will bring them positive results?

A more relatable example of employing the wrong tools for an important job is the act of feeding one's body toxic junk food when in reality the body requires a wide array of nutritional substances to thrive. Another example is the choice to think negative or limiting thoughts while trying to build a successful business or embarking on a creative endeavor. In both situations a positive and expansive outlook is essential to success. It follows along this line of thinking that numbing oneself with alcohol, drugs, food, sex or work—rather than heeding the soul's sacred call to grow and live with purpose—hinders the power of your natural toolset is always available.

One's natural toolset, otherwise known as the mind, body and spirit, are always available to use. These powerful tools are more than sufficient to tackle any task regardless of the size. Consider this reminder: when it comes to pursuing a life of true success, your toolset is your gifts, which are already within. So why is it that most people seem to forget how incredibly capable and resourceful they already are? The answer to this question lies in the three words that people shun the most: taking personal responsibility (also known as TPR).

The Freedom to Begin

> *"Do not believe in anything simply because you have heard it. Do not believe in anything simply because it's spoken and rumored by many. Do not believe in anything simply because it's found written in your religious books. Do not believe in anything merely on the authority of your teachers and elders. Do not believe in traditions because they have been handed down for many generations. But after observation and analysis, when you find that anything agrees with reason and is conducive to the good and benefit of one and all, then accept it and live up to it."*
> ~ Buddha

How often do your friends, family members, co-workers, and you complain about the problematic forces that make life a challenge? Do you feel that you're consumed by the common complaint that you have no natural luck? Or perhaps you're obsessed by the obstacles of the difficult economy and blame the outside world for your lack of success? While we can earnestly acknowledge that unfortunate things often happen to good people, it's also a universal truth that the decision to be accountable for the outcome of your life will bring about much more powerful results than complaints or self-pity. The trajectory of one's life can be altered through positive action and thinking, and through a process of engaging with the inner workings of your mind, body and spirit.

You can change your life for the better, and you have the freedom to choose to start this process of personal renaissance today. Take a moment to evaluate the powerful tools that you have available to you, and decide to utilize them to their full abilities. You possess the same instruments as all successful people. We all work within the same time constraints, living and breathing 24 hours a day, 365 days a year. Each among us has a mind, body and spirit with which to achieve success, personal fulfillment and enlightenment.

Taking personal responsibility is the critical first step to living a life of true success, yet the extent to which you take responsibility is governed by how conscious, awake and self-aware you allow yourself to be. Awareness of TPR is on a continuum. Blame and victimhood rest at one end of the spectrum, with personal responsibility located at the opposite end, and consciousness firmly planted in the middle.

As we discuss the vast range of potential awareness, I encourage you to remember: *where you choose to be positioned along the continuum is completely up to you!*

❋ SELF-ASSESSMENT

The personal responsibility spectrum is:

Blame/Victimhood ⟷ Personal Responsibility

♦ Where are you on the spectrum of taking personal responsibility for your life?

♦ Is there an area (inner-self: relationship with self or outer-self: physical, work, family societal) in your life where you are not taking personal responsibility?

Record your answers in your journal.

Chapter 4:

Let Go

"Perfection is not a prerequisite to greatness."
~ Arianna Huffington

Metaphorically, I stand at the edge of the cliff, looking down. I ready myself for the leap into the unknown, spreading my arms and holding my head high. I let go of the familiar and trust that where I land is where I am meant to be.

Letting go, free falling, trusting that you will always be taken care of, having all of your needs met and your heart's desires fulfilled sounds so simple, doesn't it? Rest assured, it's that simple. When you let go of attachments (manifestations of ego) to people, places, things, and expectations, you free yourself to explore hidden aspects of yourself and to explore life on a deeper and more meaningful level. Letting go implies trusting, and it's in that tiny space of trust where your life can blossom larger than you ever imagined. In essence, upgrading from the stifling energy of *expectation* to the more relaxed and fun energy of *exploration* will help lift worry, fear and doubt from your thoughts and therefore, from your physical body. The very idea of an exploration speaks to allowing for events and experiences to unfold exactly how they naturally will, rather than expecting a certain outcome. Having certain expectations can limit your experiences.

Think about the idea of expectation and apply it to one's need of having everything be perfect. For example, let's say you expect everything you do to be perfect. If that is the case then chances are you'll never be satisfied, nor will you experience the beauty that often comes from imperfection. Perfectionism is a creation of ego, designed to keep you stuck and unable to complete projects and move forward. At the very least, striving for perfection will limit the joy you experience that naturally comes from allowing your experience to unfold. However, at the very most, striving for perfection (when it comes to your creative endeavors) will not allow their brilliance to see the light of day because they will never be good enough or perfect enough!

A much easier and more productive approach comes when you focus on progress rather than perfection. Give it a try; I think you'll agree.

The process of letting go is a simple one, since it's easy to say, "Okay, that's it universe. I give up. You handle this for me, will ya?" However, getting to that point is another matter altogether. For most, surrendering or letting go is preceded by worry, angst, fear, anxiety, and many other not-so-pleasant emotions, but it doesn't have to be that way.

Oprah and **The Color Purple**

Oprah knows this all too well. Early in her career she came across the book *The Color Purple*. Reading the first few lines of the book deeply resonated with her to the point she felt like she was reading her own story. A few months after reading the book she heard it was going to be made into a movie, and intuitively she knew somehow she was going to play a part in the movie. Oprah said, "I was obsessed about this story, obsessed about it! I ate, slept, and thought all the time about *The Color Purple*. I moved to Chicago. I get a call from a casting agent asking if I would like to audition for a movie. I've never got a call in my life from anybody for a movie or anything like that, and I say, 'Is this *The Color Purple*?'"

"And he says, 'No, it's a movie called *Moon Song*.'

"And I go, 'Well I've been praying for *The Color Purple*.' And I go to the audition and of course it was *The Color Purple*. I audition, I don't hear anything for months and I go to this fat farm and I think it's because I'm fat I was 212 pounds at that time. And I think I didn't get the call back because I'm so fat. And I'm at this fat farm, and I'm praying and crying. Saying to God, help me let this go because I wanted to be in this movie so much, I wanted it, I wanted it, I wanted it, I thought I was going to be in the movie, there are all these signs I should be in the movie and I go to this fat farm and I'm praying and crying and as I'm on the track singing the song: I surrender all, I surrender all, all to thee my blessed savior. I surrender all.

"I'm singing that song, praying and crying, a woman comes out to me and she says, on the track, it's raining, and she says, there's a phone call for you. And the phone call was Steven Spielberg saying: 'I want to see you in my office, in California tomorrow.'"(Curry, Ann article, *Oprah comes full circle*, 2006)

In the very moment Oprah surrendered her own will and let go, she allowed fate to intervene and unseen invisible forces stepped in and delivered.

Having the ability to let go with ease and grace comes after you become conscious and aware that something in your life, internally such as a way of being, thinking or acting is no longer serving you. Letting go also applies to external factors such as people, places, things and experiences in your life that no longer serve your highest and best.

Once awareness is achieved, next comes quieting ego and not allowing it to interfere. Ego, as previously mentioned is a trickster and will do its best to make you believe you need to hold onto people, places and things that no longer serve you, and let go of what does serve you.

Then, after becoming aware and quieting the ego... follow your heart! If deep in your heart you feel something is truly right for you, honor yourself by following your passion and stay the course... trust everything is working out in your favor.

The next step is a bit tricky because this is where most get confused, yet it's also where "the rubber meets the road" when it comes to manifesting your desires.

Ready? Okay here it goes:

> *When you accept and allow for*
> *what is meant to be will be...*
> *you set yourself free!*

This confuses some people because they interpret *accepting* to mean *giving up*. When I share this secret with business people who haven't yet embraced their higher consciousness, this altered way of thinking drives them nuts. Why does it drive them nuts? Because they're being willful and want things to work out *how* they want them to, rather than being open to other more magical and meaningful ways for their life to unfold. They haven't yet opened up to how simple, joyful and amazing life can be when they learn to trust and let go!

I'll give you an example. During the summer of 2007 my brother (then realtor) was on a hot streak when it came to his real estate sales, and he had over $50,000 in the bank. He was excited, and of course he wanted to spend the money. So he started looking at bigger houses that were in his neighborhood. After a few weeks of searching, he found a home two blocks from where he lived that was perfect for him and his family. It was almost three times the square footage of the house he lived in, and it had a pool. The price tag was $600,000. The home they lived in then probably would have sold for $250,000, and it had little equity. So after it was all said and done he would have had all his money tied up in the new big home plus a mortgage close to $500,000. Oh, and the taxes on the new home were over $16,000 a year, compared to the $1,900 in taxes on the home they lived in.

I told him not to do it. He got upset with me. He put an offer in on the house and waited to hear back. Within a week he called me complaining that the realtor who had the listing didn't submit his offer in time and had sold the house to someone else. Needless to say, he was really upset. I told him what he disliked hearing most from me, "Relax, it wasn't meant to be. Maybe you can't see the reason now, but you will later."

Two weeks later he called to tell me he had been diagnosed with stage-four colon cancer. Thankfully, he had money in savings, and he and his family were still in their comfortable and affordable home.

Now, let's get back to Oprah's story because she left out a few very significant details from the quote above regarding her experience of getting a lead role in the movie *The Color Purple*. Here they are:

While Oprah was running around the track singing and crying, she was deciding whether or not she could stomach seeing the movie if someone else played the role of Sophia. At first she thought no, she couldn't do it; yet as she continued around the track singing, praying, and releasing, she warmed up to the idea of it being okay for her to see the movie. The longer she ran, the more she prayed to God—until she finally got to the point of accepting that not only could she see the movie with someone else playing "her" role, but that she would actually be happy for the person who was playing the role of Sophia. It was in that moment she got the phone call from Stephen Spielberg who said, "I heard you were at a fat farm. You better have not lost a pound or you might lose your part in the movie." Oprah left the fat farm and stopped at Dairy Queen on the way home to replace any calories she might have lost at the fat farm.

There are several amazing things about this story. First, the only reason Oprah was at the fat farm was because she thought she didn't get a role in the movie because she was too fat, which we know wasn't true based on Stephen Spielberg's comment to her.

Second, rather than mentally beating herself up about her weight, had Oprah just stayed in Chicago doing her thing and trusting that what was meant to happen would, when Steven Spielberg called she would probably have been home enjoying dinner rather than at a fat farm running in the rain.

And third, Oprah had to completely let go, surrender, accept, and feel grateful for the opportunity to see the movie regardless of her involvement. So, ask yourself, "Am I currently living my life aligned with my truth, or am I living my life based on what I think I should be doing…out of fear?"

Gratitude and Clear Intentions

Oprah's story illustrates the power of having *crystal-clear* intentions, which are another form of prayer transmitting to the universe. Gratitude felt when sending out crystal-clear intentions always brings those things aligned with your highest and best to you. Furthermore, gratitude can be thought of as the universal retriever bringing you everything to support your highest and best, as above so below.

Now, some say, "Hey, wait a minute. I was grateful for my job, but I got fired." Well, maybe that was the universe helping you along your path because you weren't meant to continue working in that position, and you weren't about to leave your job on your own due to fear. The more stuck we are in life, the more the universe will take matters into its own hands and create situations and opportunities to help us get unstuck. The same thing happens when someone is overworked and won't take holidays, and all of a sudden they get a sickness that forces them to stop working, to take a break and to breathe.

My intention through this book is to wake you up to the powerful forces available to you from the universe. And I want to help you understand how incredibly connected your mind, body, and spirit are in this journey. In fact, your mind, body, and spirit can be thought of as a mobile—you know, those things that hang above babies' cribs. What happens when you move a piece on that mobile? Yes, all the others move too, and the same process happens with you. When your thoughts are focused on moving toward your higher purpose or life's mission, then your subconscious mind gets alerted to what you're looking to experience. Your subconscious mind then tells your body what to look out for. Lastly, your body communicates (via your gut feelings) which steps to take for your desired experience to manifest. The process is truly amazing and works with everything and anything.

You just have to learn how to let go, trust the process and get out of your own way.

Letting go implies trusting in your abilities and in the universe to deliver what you desire in your life. Uncertainty and confusion prevail when you hold onto and follow old ideas, thoughts, or beliefs that no longer serve you.

Faith and Fear

As I previously mentioned, faith and fear can't coexist, which means at all times, you're either operating from a place of *faith* or *fear*. The choice to become conscious and aware of when you're coming from faith or fear is essential for you to experience true success.

For instance, let's say you have just been laid off and are actually quite happy about it since you have always wanted to start a business of your own, and you view losing your job as an opportunity to do just that. Great, you're off to a terrific start and are firmly entrenched in the faith camp! However, after a month or so, you aren't seeing the results that you wanted (namely, the money isn't coming to you as quickly as you thought it would), and you begin to second-guess your decision-making ability and your ability to build your own business. Doubt starts to creep into your daily life, and instead of building your own business by making more contacts, you spend time searching job postings. Soon your daily activity becomes based in fear, and has nothing to do with building your own business and all momentum is lost. Your own business eludes you, and you end up taking any job to get your bills paid.

The moment you switched from building your business to searching for a job, you told the universe you really weren't sincere about building your business. However, people who sincerely know deep within that they want to start their own business and will do whatever it takes to become successful, invite to themselves all seen and unseen forces to aid in making their dreams come true. The process is scary, though, because you have to let go of your fears and trust that things are going to work out long before evidence of this becomes apparent.

That's why I say "trust" is a verb, not a noun. You have to take action regardless of what is being presented to you this very moment. You see, just as a seed is planted in the soil, even though your eyes can't see, its foundation is being nourished for its roots to grow and spread. The gardener knows and trusts that the seed will eventually bear fruit in the form of a flower, fruit, tree, lettuce or vegetable... as will your ideas, thoughts and visions grow and flourish.

To Catch, You Must Send

How does letting go work? Energetically what you let go of, lets go of you and returns more to you. Consider a game of Frisbee. If you don't let go of the Frisbee, can your friend receive it? No. Now what if she doesn't let go of the Frisbee—can you receive it? No, you both must engage in letting go and in receiving in order to have any fun playing Frisbee.

Unlike playing Frisbee, sometimes letting go can be painful. This is why people have difficulty letting go. They don't want to experience pain. What they haven't realized is that the very act of letting go allows them to experience more. Letting go of the past is a necessary step toward becoming fully present and receiving all that your heart desires. Letting go of things, people, places and old thoughts will not only liberate your soul; it will also help you step into a life of freedom. You'll feel more alive, awake and empowered to receive all that your heart desires.

It's really that simple.

I wrestled with holding on tightly to those things I thought brought me happiness. I quickly learned that once the newness of material possessions wore off, I still felt empty inside. Filling an inner void with everything from food to expensive cars wasn't cutting it. Soon I found myself with no other choice than to let go of those things I thought were feeding my soul. Trust me when I tell you, if you don't do the work to figure out *why* you hold onto things, you will never fully heal your addiction *to* things. Because you will make yourself believe you are holding onto things for a good reason, rather than getting to the real reason you hold onto things that no longer serve you. When observing the people, places and things in your life, ask yourself this one very important question:

> *"Does this (insert noun)*
> *serve my highest and best?"*
> *If the answer is no, let it go!*

When you allow yourself to let go, you say to the universe, "I trust." The universe responds to your message of trusting by enhancing your life with an abundance of love, joy, freedom, happiness, prosperity, and anything else your heart desires.

Now, you might be thinking, "Wait a second, I let go of an unhappy relationship last week … now where are all the gifts the universe has for me?" Trust me, they're coming. Keep reading, and stay the course by believing and trusting that good things are coming to you.

From Your Head to Your Heart

The moment you decide to let go, freedom is achieved and your energy shifts to a higher vibration that transcends ego, connecting you to the place inside where you commune with the Source. At that moment, you'll have completed the longest 16-inch journey of your life: you'll have moved from your head to your heart. Those of you who have already made the journey from your head to your heart arc thinking, "Yeah, that feels right," but those who are still in their heads are thinking, "How does he know it's sixteen inches from my head to my heart?" Dropping down from your head to your heart is easy for some and difficult for many. For those of you who are logical thinkers, this exercise may be challenging.

A few years ago at a workshop I held, a memorable attendee who owned her own business struggled to let go. She found it really difficult to let herself be vulnerable and allow herself to stop analyzing and to start feeling. I worked to assist her to find what she was passionate about. I gently probed with questions about her interests and her passions, yet nothing seemed to connect her to her heart. However, when I asked about her children, the tears started flowing. Although her children were grown, the very mention of them allowed her to move from her conscious thinking mind, *her head*, and go right to her feeling place, *her heart.*

Why is it important to go from your head to your heart?

First, you attract success more quickly when you allow feelings such as gratitude, joy, compassion and love to fill you up and to engage your integral, trusting self.

Second, you stop your ego from running the show, since its job is to keep you small, fearful, disempowered and limited. It does so by telling you lies about yourself every day. Your heart is more powerful than your mind, and your ego only has access to your mind, not your heart.

Third, you can begin to receive communication from your sixth sense when you're in your heart. Your sixth sense is your inner knowing, and communicates with you through your feelings, your gut instincts and your intuition. We'll go deeper into this in Chapter 13.

Ego

You've heard the saying "What you resist, persists." There's a flip side to that: "What you look into dissolves." It's not necessary to push away or ignore your ego; you must first embrace it and make friends with it. Friends like to be acknowledged. In order to acknowledge your ego, start by noticing when it's trying to run the show. You'll know your ego has taken over when you feel afraid, beat yourself up for something that you said or did, or when you're thinking of yourself and others in an unkind way. The moment you realize your ego has taken over, stop whatever it is you're doing and focus on your breath. While breathing, think about something or someone who makes you happy, and allow for those thoughts or feelings to expand to the point you're smiling from the inside out. Feelings of gratitude, in fact, are the quickest way to quiet the ego and to tap into your sixth sense. Other ways are through humor, feelings of joy, smiling, exercising, meditating, and becoming present in the moment rather than thinking about the past or future.

To go deeper in meditation, my students and I find it helpful to silence ego. The following is a way to remove ego before meditating and before connecting to your inner knowing.

When relaxed, bring to mind a visual of your ego. Mine comes to me in the form of a large black figure that resembles the Michelin tire man. I ask my ego, nicely and gently, to please leave through a nearby door. More often than not my ego chooses to stay, so I resort to visualizing two guards who look similar to the Beefeaters who stand guard at Buckingham Palace dressed in their black hats and red coats. I then watch as the guards escort my ego out the door, and then stand guard to ensure my ego stays away while I meditate. Ever since I started escorting my ego out the door, my meditations have deepened and my ability to receive information through my intuition has increased. I hope you find the same happens for you when you use the ego exiting visualization. For further exploration of ego, visit Eckhart Tolle's work.

Getting to the Heart of the Matter

Many rewards come when you allow yourself to move from your conscious-thinking mind (head) into your heart. First, you will have access to the most powerful manifesting tool available: your feelings. Your feelings can be thought of as vibrational waves sending vehicles into the universe and bringing you what your heart desires. These vibrational waves act like boomerangs by bringing back to you a vibrational match of how you're feeling. In other words, feeling good will bring you experiences that will allow you to continue to feel good. Feeling bad, frustrated or sad, on the other hand, will bring you experiences that will still leave you feeling bad, frustrated or sad. Remember, what you put out, you get back.

I tried an experiment to test this theory. Every morning for a week, as soon as I woke up I made a conscious choice to feel a certain way, and I then projected that feeling out and into the universe as I was interacting with people. The first morning I purposely chose to feel happy, and my smile clearly communicated that feeling. Most people I walked past that day returned the smile, and my day clipped along beautifully, giving me many experiences that allowed me to continue feeling happy.

However, the next morning I purposely chose to feel sad. What a difference that made! Very few people smiled at me, and my day became so tedious that by the end of it I was almost in tears.

I needed to change the vibe, so the next day I chose to feel relaxed by slowing down my usual fast pace, saying hello first to people I encountered and even stopping to chat with them. By doing so, I found that people responded to me in a similar way. I even attracted two hugs from complete strangers! It became apparent to me that what we project out and into the universe does have a direct impact on what we experience in life.

Inspired, I decided to ramp up my experiment and add the power of my thoughts to my feelings, to see what I could manifest. The following day, I chose to feel completely open to receiving, feeling happy and joyful, combined with the conscious thought that "Today is my day." That morning I jumped out of bed and into the shower. As I showered, I thought about receiving a free chai tea latte. That was my goal. I headed downtown to the local coffee shop, and sure enough, I ran into a buddy who said, "Let me buy you a drink." Now, the amazing part of this story is that he was ahead of me in line and there were two people between us, so he had to look behind, spot me and feel compelled to buy me a drink. After that day, I started thinking more about what I could accomplish by my intentions, conscious thoughts and feelings all of course while experimenting.

This strategy works for everything such as attracting my soul mate, having amazing experiences while traveling internationally, parking, conducting seminars, coaching, writing, meditating, vacationing.... It just takes a little work ahead of time, and your "work" is: *to get clear about what you desire to attract, let go of expectations, get out of your head, drop down into your heart, and feel gratitude for the things you desire to come to you before they come.*

Easy, right? Of course it is—you don't have to take my word that this works. I encourage you to try experimenting on your own and see what works for you and then send me an email to Jaden@jadensterling.com.

I would love to hear!

A few simple tips to remember as you continue to let go:

✓ Always learn from your experiences rather than the outcome. Learning along the way will allow for a much richer journey and for miracles to happen for you.

✓ When one door closes, another one opens. Saying good-bye to people, places and things can be difficult! However, know that everything happens for you rather than to you. Trust that there is a very good reason why a door shuts.

✓ Make important decisions that will have a lasting impact only when you feel confident and are feeling good. In other words, make lasting decisions only when you're firmly entrenched in the faith camp.

✓ Let go of people, places and things after you have known in your gut for at least thirty days in a row that they are no longer a good fit for you.

✳ SELF-ASSESSMENT

◆ Stop here and take a moment to recall when you successfully visualized or imagined something that you needed, and sure enough you got it.

◆ Why did this happen? Was it because you were vibrationally in tune with the universe?

◆ What experiments can you conduct in your daily life to practice and test these skills?

◆ Are you willing to replace the desire to be perfect with making progress as you grow your current business or start a new one?

Consider doing a R.A.K. (Random Act of Kindness) daily for thirty days and see what comes back to you.

Chapter 5:
Overcome the Blame Game

"When you blame others,
you give up your power to change."
~ Anonymous

If a portrait that was anticipated to be a masterpiece turns out to be a subpar likeness, is it the fault of the model, or the fault of the artist? If your life isn't matching the dreams that you had devised, who is to blame? Is it the fault of your parents, the economy, the system, your gender, or your level of education? Could the root of the problem possibly lie within you?

The blame game is an easy trap to fall into. At some time or another we all experience lows in our lives. There are times when the struggle to improve our situation or make things better can feel almost impossible. Yet the act of perpetually placing the blame outside of us is counterproductive.

Let's figure this out, shall we? If you honestly believe your life is the way it is because you have been dealt a "bad hand," then you've placed the ability to have an amazing life outside of your control. When something exists outside of you, do you have the ability to change it? Probably not, but when something exists within you, how easily can you change it? Easily, right? Yes, and you do so by taking personal responsibility (TPR).

To put it in another light, the road to becoming successful will always elude you if you continue to blame someone or something for what you currently do or do not have. By doing so, you cast away your means of change; your inherent power is diminished, and this very act halts you on your path to success. Powerless people cannot make changes or determine their own fate.

On the flip side, TPR can yield abundant results if you're ready to embrace it. You just need courage to stand your ground and remain the architect of your own journey!

It can be very challenging for people to take personal responsibility for the role they play in their own lives. There are many reasons for this, yet it's often due to one of two things: either the person will have to make a self-motivated change (and people aren't fond of change) or they will become immobilized by fear, which doesn't allow for action. Whether you're firmly entrenched in the blame game, or you're the type of person who always takes personal responsibility for your actions, these steps can help you. An understanding of TPR can guide you or someone you know to reach the heart of this matter, and begin to heal.

Reclaim Your Power

The most challenging part of stopping the blame game that dominates so many lives is being able to recognize this unproductive behavior when it occurs. The first essential step to ending the habit is to identify the thought patterns that cause a shift of personal responsibility away from oneself. The very act of not blaming others for your place in life is a simple first step. This puts you in the driver's seat rather than in the back seat. Living in the back seat allows others to take you where *they* want you to go, which is fine if that is how you want to live your life.

Remember, when you point the finger at someone and blame them for your challenges, you have three more fingers pointing back at you!

Start heeding the message of those three fingers, and look at the role you play in your own life. I remember a time when I thought it was my girlfriend's (now wife) responsibility to make me happy. Looking back, I chuckle now as my query on Google comes to mind; I would type into the search engine: "Who is responsible for my happiness?" It was an answer that Google could not generate. I learned, after much angst, that I was solely responsible for fulfilling my needs and it wasn't someone else's responsibility to make me happy! Furthermore, I learned that others are responsible for themselves as well, and that I could only take care of myself as best I could to make the world a better place. The act of taking responsibility for myself, while releasing my need to be responsible for the happiness of others, was a huge relief.

The next step to reclaiming your power is to stop the blame game. In order to stop blaming others, you must become aware of when you're engaging in this negative behavior. To make the process easier, consider enlisting the support of family and friends by sharing your thoughts on this matter with them. Explain that you're on a new path to success and are working to release unproductive habits and improve your skills at overcoming obstacles as they arise. Then ask your loved ones to bring to your attention each time they notice you engaging in the blame game. Their view from the outside is a valuable asset that can shave time and struggle from your growth process. One way to enlist people's engagement with your process is to offer them a nominal sum of money every time they catch you not taking personal responsibility by blaming other people, places or things. Obviously the more money you offer, the more closely they'll be listening to your words and evaluating your actions.

Despite your best efforts, the process of rooting out this unproductive behavior will take some time to master. If in the heat of the moment you catch yourself engaging in the blame game, take a moment of quiet reflection. Stop talking, take a deep breath, and when you're able to, affirm something empowering rather than blaming. For example, perhaps your standard response to the question, "How's business?" has recently been anything but positive, placing responsibility on the outside world and the economy, rather than on yourself. If you wish to change your attitude and prepare yourself for TPR, you could replace your previous answer with the affirmation: "Business keeps getting better each day." This choice to implement a positive answer is far more empowering of a response than blaming the economy. The act of participating in a positive daily dialogue will lighten your heart and mind, and prepare your soul to take on even more challenging work.

As you begin the process of reclaiming your power, you may be wondering why this act is so paramount to success. We have already discussed the fact that reconnecting to your own personal power is essential for you to experience success on every level in life. When we talk about personal power within this context, we are by no means referring to perceived power that's rooted in ego. The kind of power that needs to be harnessed for spiritual success has nothing to do with ego and everything to do with truth of heart.

> *Genuine power allows one to be*
> *authentic rather than popular.*

Being authentic allows you to stand up for what you know is right, even when everyone else thinks and feels differently. This power allows you to trust yourself, others and the universe to fulfill your needs. This power allows you to engage with and live a fulfilling life. This same power will assist you to strive beyond your personal wants and embark upon a pilgrimage of service to others who have greater needs.

By deciding to abandon the blame game, you're able to reach out and take possession of this magnificent power, already completely contained within yourself. It's a power that connects you to the creator of everything, and that connection takes place inside you. Science tells us this is the area of your brain called the pineal gland, often referred to as the gateway to consciousness or God Center. This wealth of capability and connection allows you complete access to genius, clarity, focus, inspiration and passion.

At a basic level for every human, this immense power comes from within and is not based upon external factors. With the blame game that distracted you for so long fading away into the past, you're in a prime position to experiment with the next essential step along your journey. It's time to become conscious, and learn to be in the moment.

✳ SELF-ASSESSMENT

♦ Bring to mind a recent experience where something frustrating happened in your life and you blamed others for it. After carefully examining the event, can you now see your role in how it unfolded?

♦ Is there anything that you're aware of that stops you from taking personal responsibility for your life?

♦ What could you do to take more responsibility for your happiness?

♦ How do you affect change into your life by taking personal responsibility?

Chapter 6:
How Conscious Are You?

"Consciousness is the ultimate reality."
~ Deepak Chopra

Delving into the immense field of consciousness is similar to diving headfirst into the deep blue sea: the vastness is awe-inspiring and both realms are best explored while wearing a headlamp and flippers. Okay, perhaps you won't need flippers to expand your consciousness; however, a metaphorical headlamp might come in handy, as it could serve to light your path and help you to become more aware.

Consciousness is essential to our exploration because it's the middle ground between placing blame and TPR. In other words, one cannot take full responsibility for their actions until the threshold of consciousness is crossed. But in order to pass into this important realm of self-discovery, we first must understand exactly what it is that we are seeking.

So, what is consciousness? Consciousness is your ability to process experiences (internally and externally) and become aware of the effect they have on you. Quite simply, consciousness is your way of waking up to how you are being affected by everything that happens inside of you and outside of you. I recall a time while writing this book when I experienced a heightened sense of consciousness that was brought on by the experience of running. I've already shared how eating became a favorite past time of mine while writing this book which led to me gain excess weight. Yet, it wasn't until I started running that I became conscious of how the excess weight was affecting my knees and my body. Thankfully, due to my experience of running and the huffing and puffing that went along with it, I immediately became conscious of the effect my choice of excess eating had on my body. Thus, it is fair to say that consciousness is a state of being that comes when you are aware of how events affect you *internally*.

Your internal processing of external events allows you to further your awakening and deepen your awareness. This is a process of taking action and becoming aware of what is working for you in life and what is not working for you. Therefore, consciousness can be thought of as a verb rather than a noun.

Being conscious allows you to be in touch with the central truths that govern your life and body, which allow you to make the best possible choices for yourself regarding all aspects of your life, at all times.

Although most seek to become more conscious and believe it's difficult, the truth is that in opening yourself up to the experience, the process unfolds naturally. For example, imagine that you're driving down the road and your conscious thinking mind is focused on a project you are working on back at the office. Suddenly, in a split second a deer leaps out in front of your car. Now, is having the awareness of a deer jumping in front of your car enough to effect change? No. You must take action and your impulses take over. You slam on the brakes and swerve in order to successfully miss hitting the deer. The formula for increasing consciousness is similar to this, and it's rather simple. You must undertake a pattern of being, doing, being, doing, and so on.

Awareness precedes consciousness.

We can all relate to the experience of feeling disconnected from the present. You're somewhere important, engaged in daily life, and the next thing you know your thoughts have drifted somewhere else to another place and time. This kind of habit is a basic human behavior, however this does not make it productive. While reading, many people find themselves "spacing out," allowing interfering memories or worries to detract from the pleasure of the experience. The experience of reading and relaxing is diminished because of the distractions of the mind.

If you can relate to these common problems, it's important to take hold of your consciousness right now! Let's investigate the steps to waking up your awareness. You can become really present and cognizant of what you're doing in this very moment, which is the first step to becoming conscious.

Many readers may be wondering, "How do I know if I am truly aware?"

Going through life unaware is common, and it's certainly a habit that some people are more prone to than others. Performing habitual tasks, without pleasure or sensation, and living a life that's set to autopilot is not unusual. Existing in an unconscious zone of being can delude you for a considerable amount of time; however, unless you change your behavior and thus become conscious, you'll not grow spiritually, emotionally or financially.

If you're unsure about your level of consciousness, you may want to take a momentary assessment of your inner connectivity by asking yourself the following questions:

- What are the approximate number of tasks you perform each day *routinely* rather than *consciously*?
- How many times have you driven to a familiar destination and when you arrived you couldn't remember the drive there?
- How often do you catch yourself during the course of the day feeling forgetful or unfocused?
- How often do you find yourself not listening to others as they talk?
- How many times during the course of the day do you allow your mind to wander to unproductive thoughts?

- How often do you do something solely because it's the way you've always done it, or because others do it that way?
- Do you strive to improve how you do things or are you more comfortable doing things the same way all the time?
- Are you open to constructive ideas?
- Can you see the role you play in how your life is unfolding or do you blame others for your experiences?

Consider the above questions and answer them truthfully. Being honest with yourself increases your chances of becoming conscious, which in turn will allow you to make new and better choices that can impact your life in positive ways. Making such positive decisions will allow you to change your experiences, and when your experiences change for the better, so does your life.

Consciousness Is A Choice

We all live in this world that holds infinite choices. We are free to choose our paths much more than we have been led to believe.

The same tenets of choice and freedom apply to the art of consciousness. It's your personal decision whether or not to deeply engage in the act of waking up and recommencing your life in every moment.

Awareness > Consciousness > Presence

People who feel that they must be attached to their PDAs at every moment of the day, even if they are spending valuable time with friends and loved ones, are making a very serious choice to be *busy* over being *present* in the important moments of their lives that may not come again.

The choice to engage with being conscious and present in the moment is truly yours to make every second of every day. It is easy to be unconscious. When you challenge yourself to be conscious and present each moment, you will have the strength to make changes in your life.

You may have already gathered that journeying along the path of true success requires you to show up and be conscious. If your life is complicated to the point that living presently is simply not possible most of the time, it's important to understand why the choice to be busy has taken precedence over your ability to be a whole and grounded being.

If all of this sounds intriguing, then you're ready to begin, and you're likely already aching to know the answer to our next essential question: "How may I become more conscious and aware?"

The path toward personal consciousness requires you to take a series of interdependent steps, many of which involve self-introspection. Self-introspection is a rewarding process that starts when you become aware of why you do what you do. The journey deepens when you become aware of your thoughts, beliefs and the effects that your actions have on yourself, others, and the planet.

Everyone and Everything Are One

Imagine yourself as just one being in this enormous world of motion, pleasure and beauty. Recall that you're simply one of many, but also remember that everything and everyone are connected. We all share the surface of our planet; we all eat and breathe and sleep; and we all experience pain and joy and loss and grace. We all have an individual purpose for our being, a separate drive and life force that propels us onward.

We're all here for a special reason.

Do not feel that you must change your world in huge strokes because it's the small changes that pile on top of one another that will begin to re-form the way that you view consciousness and your place in the world. We are breathing, living, human beings with a will and spirit that can guide us if we allow ourselves to be open.

This realization came to me once during my search for self-awareness. I had been experimenting with opening my mind to the transition that consciousness and self-knowing brings, and I happened to observe a line of ants productively marching across my kitchen counter. Prior to becoming conscious, I found myself doing the unthinkable—wiping them out in one swift swoop, without thinking of their purpose, or viewing them as living beings. Due to the work in my spiritual sphere that I had been engaging in, this particular morning was different. I was awake and aware, and I decided that no longer would I identify as an ant killer. Allowing them to live gave me tremendous peace in my soul. From that morning on, I led by example, and the universe gave me plenty of opportunities to share my new found enlightenment with others.

One particular morning the universe gave me the opportunity to lead by example and show what being awake and aware was all about. I was traveling, and I went to the airport and boarded my flight. Shortly after takeoff we were prompted that the captain had deemed it safe to use electronics, and so I reached for my laptop. I extended my tray table, and lo and behold a single ant paraded across the surface! I stared in utter amazement, wondering how the ant got on the plane. The gentlemen next to me saw the ant too, and he slowly reached over, with his finger extended to end its life.

Instinctively, I blocked his hand, looked him in the eye, and asked, "Who are we to end its life?" The man was stunned. He removed his finger, looked at me sideways and without saying a word continued reading his book. Silently, I laughed to myself thinking how perfect the universe is to those who seek to respect it. Perhaps in the future, that passenger who was seated next to me will choose to serve as a catalyst for someone else's journey and assist in awakening them to the beauty that comes from living consciously.

✳ SELF-ASSESSMENT

♦ How aware are you of your actions and the effect they have on yourself and others?

♦ Close your eyes and see yourself as one of many. Imagine your body and spirit sharing space with all of the other humans on the surface of the Earth. Imagine your connection. What do you feel is your special place within the universe?

Chapter 7:

Be Present in the Moment

"Do not dwell in the past, do not dream of the future;
concentrate the mind on the present moment."
~ Buddha

There is a sign that hangs on the wall in many English pubs. It declares: "Free beer tomorrow." Take some time and really think about the merit of that offer. Does anyone ever get free beer?

It's only in the present moment—the space in time between the past and the future—during which you can take action and truly make changes in your life. I enjoy the saying, "Tomorrow is a mystery, yesterday is history, and the present is truly a gift." Truth be told, the present moment is all you have to work with and it's your greatest asset in being able to effect change in your life. However, most people waste a lot of time reaching for the past with nostalgic notions and looking to the future to fulfill their dreams. In doing so, they're completely missing out on the magnificent gifts that the present has to offer.

> *Awareness is cultivated when your thoughts and actions are aligned with the here and now.*

Some of you might be feeling overwhelmed by the huge number of thoughts that you experience everyday. This is valid considering the fact that on average, a person has over 70,000 thoughts each day. So how can one ever become aware of all those thoughts? The good news is you don't have to be aware of all of them; you need only be aware of those thoughts that either pull you into the past or into the future.

So, which thoughts are those? You may find those that are rooted in fear and worry crop up most often. The easiest way to eliminate worry is first to be aware when it's happening, and second, to take action. Most people worry because they aren't taking action toward solving their current challenge in life. In other words, whatever you're worried about diminishes after you take solid steps toward finding a solution to your obstacle. Three steps or actions taken daily for 30 days will transform your life. Luckily, it won't take 30 days for you to start feeling the positive effects that this action plan can have in your life; you'll actually start seeing transformative effects *immediately.*

Feeling Gratitude

> *Be grateful for*
> *what you already have right NOW.*

Do you want to instantly transform your experience, stop worrying, and change your life for the better through consciousness? There is one little secret that is more powerful than you can imagine: The feeling of gratitude connects you to your heart, and your heart is the most electrically and magnetically powered organ in your body, trumping your brain by a magnetic factor of 5,000. Furthermore, the effects of feeling gratitude and love emit energy that has been measured and extends over two kilometers outside of your body.

Chances are you've heard the saying "like attracts like," which is how you attract what you experience. In other words, what you're emitting through your feelings and thoughts is continually being sent out into the universe and is bringing you back something in alignment with the energy you're sending out. We'll discuss this more in later chapters, but it's an important principle to keep in mind as you begin your process of change.

At this point, I think it should be clear that I am not an advocate for having more stuff for the sake of having stuff or status. Rather, I am in favor of increasing the quality of your life and your experiences through organic means. I urge you to give yourself completely to every moment and every experience now because now is all you have. Avoid distractions from your phone or laptop, and be present with your family and friends. Be more attentive, creative and mindful at work while you're there, and don't allow for distractions.

These simple changes can have a huge impact on your quality of life and on your ability to experience true success. Ask yourself: "Can I really have the experience of success in my personal and professional life when I have difficulty being present because my thoughts are continuously being diverted elsewhere?" Now can you begin to see the benefits from becoming conscious and aware? If what I'm saying resonates with you, let's go deeper and explore the part of you that controls 95% of your thoughts: the subconscious.

The Unconscious and Subconscious Mind

Understanding the subtle differences between the unconscious, subconscious, and conscious mind is essential for your success. Consciousness, as we have already explored, is the act of being present, lucid, and aware of yourself in the moment. Unconsciousness is a state of being that provides vital functions independently of present consciousness (example is when you do anything routinely or repeatedly). Your subconscious exists under the conscious mind and represents the place where memories, often a deeper motivation, are stored.

All of these elements interact to compose the way that your mind makes sense of the world and navigates your day-to-day life. For example, when you're driving down the street, it's common for your mind to wander over any number of topics, such as what you're going to make for dinner that night (not my wife's first thought). Clearly, your conscious thoughts are not fixed on driving, yet you're still able to maneuver the car. This is because your subconscious takes control of the situation, allowing you to complete the function required in the current moment through the memory of how it's done. The unconscious mind allows you to go through your days fully functioning and on autopilot while the conscious mind is focused elsewhere. Every experience you have leaves an imprint in your unconscious memory. Your unconscious mind makes quick judgments and can deem whether a person is worthy or competent. This is how you process nonverbal communication, which is automatic and powerful. However, your conscious mind doesn't even have time to get involved. The conscious mind switches on when it comes to new or important things, and can only handle input from four or five things at a time.

Your unconscious mind brings to your attention that which you focus on. For example, have you ever noticed when you consciously make up your mind to buy a certain make and model of car, you begin to see that type of car everywhere? While the same make and model of that particular vehicle was always in your view, your unconscious mind didn't think it was important to bring your attention to it. It's only when you assert your awareness that you begin to take notice.

When you have an experience, you truly believe that your experience is new and immediate. However, what's actually happening is that you're processing the past from projected memory. Your eyes allow for input, just as a lens on a camera allows for an image to be processed or photographed; yet the lens is not taking the picture. Similarly, your eyes are not processing the image you're seeing either. The image you take in through your eyes gets filtered through your visual cortex and is not in real time but rather is being projected from memory.

This is why it's imperative to spend time visualizing the kind of life you desire regardless of your current situation. Your brain and body are so powerful that you have the ability to override what you visually see with what you *desire* to see. For example, you are looking at your bank statement seeing $1,000. However, choosing to see a balance of $10,000 on your statement will help bring that to you. This process allows for the images that you hold within to manifest for you.

> *You draw experiences to you*
> *that are congruent with your mindset.*

If you have an abundant mindset, you'll experience more people, places and things that will reflect abundance back to you. Conversely, if you have a mindset rooted in fear and scarcity, you'll attract people, places and things that reflect the experience of lack back to you.

It's important to be selective when it comes to being conscious. Attempting to be conscious every moment of every day can exhaust you and deplete you of your carnal energy, since conscious thinking takes more energy. Therefore, the goal of a successful and enlightened life can be reached by being *selectively* conscious. There is much talk about the importance of becoming conscious. However, due to the fact that your subconscious controls 95% of your thoughts and therefore your behavior, I believe it's more important to focus on your subconscious so it is in alignment with your conscious desires. The flow evolves as such:

Unconscious
(handles vital bodily
functions & routine tasks)

Conscious
(presence, awareness)

Subconscious
(stores memories
and deep awareness)

We must evaluate and understand the aspects of our life that demand sincere attention. In order to attain your dreams and goals, you'll have to assess what is truly intrinsic to your happiness. By pointing your subconscious mind in the direction that you wish for it to go, your experiences will reflect back to you what you truly desire.

Affirmations

There are several ways to either program or reprogram your subconscious. Listening to specific guided meditations on what you desire to achieve while you're in a relaxed mindset works well. I prefer to do this at bedtime, and it's advisable to maintain the routine for 30 days in a row. This will program your subconscious to seek out and bring to you people, places and things for you to experience that which you desire. Affirmations work best when said out loud while looking into a mirror. Also, the affirmations need to be said in the present tense and said as if you have already achieved your goal. For example, on my *Money: Healing Meditation and Affirmation CD* a few of the affirmations are:

- I manifest money easily and effortlessly, free and clear, here and now.
- I manifest large sums of money by the new profitable opportunities that come my way today.

These affirmations are written clearly, in the first person and in the present tense. It's simple, really, and if you want to supercharge your affirmations start with the words "I am grateful for _____ (fill in your own affirmation) blessing my life here and now."

While saying your affirmations out loud it is important to occupy your conscious thinking mind so that you can access your subconscious mind. An easy way to accomplish this is to hold your arms directly out in front of you clasping your fingers together with your thumbs next to each other pointing upwards. Now follow your thumbs with just your eyes as you move your hands in a figure-8 keeping your arms straight in front of you and keeping your head still. While moving your hands repeat your affirmations out loud. This process occupies your conscious thinking mind by using your eyes to follow your thumbs moving in the figure-8, and allows you direct access to your subconscious mind.

The reason affirmations are important to repeat over and over is because when you do they imprint on your subconscious what you truly desire. Early on in this process it might feel awkward to repeat phrases as if you've already achieved that goal, before you actually achieve it. Nevertheless, trust that affirmations work and that you deserve to achieve what you truly desire. The most important thing to keep in mind regarding any practice you engage in to further your personal development is to *believe* you can achieve your goal regardless of your present situation. Repeating phrases while looking in the mirror out loud to yourself only works when you truly believe you can achieve your goal.

Voice Your Affirmations

When imprinting your subconscious by working with guided meditations and affirmations, remember that your spoken voice imprints faster and deeper on your subconscious than someone else's voice. That's the reason I suggest you repeat your affirmations out loud. I have made available to you through my website downloadable (actual scripts) of *The Money Magnet* and *Money Manifesting Guided Meditation* I've recorded. Go to: www.thewealthquest.com/bookresources to download the scripts, and record the meditations in your own voice. If you don't want to spend time recording your own meditation that's fine. Guided meditations recorded by other people will work too; just go with meditations that are recorded by someone who has a soothing voice and a voice that resonates with you. You can find thirty second previews of most CD tracks from iTunes, which is more than enough time to figure out if the artists' voice resonates with you.

I say "resonates" because you don't want to be agitated or annoyed listening to a guided meditation. You want to be able to relax and allow the information to access your subconscious without interruption.

Being conscious while reprogramming your subconscious mind puts you in the driver's seat of your life with your hands firmly wrapped around the steering wheel. You're present and can no longer ignore the effects of your actions and thoughts on yourself, others and the planet. Your eyes are open to the magnificence of our universe and the power that you hold within. You're now aware of the impact you can make in your own life and in the lives of others.

Being present affords you the opportunity to become aware of not only why you do what you do, but also what stops you from achieving your dreams and goals. Often people create unproductive habits that distract them from what they really want to accomplish. At times it's easier to reach for a quick fix such as food, cigarettes, alcohol, shopping, or prescription medication, etc., instead of being present and working through the emotional component required for you to go deeper within yourself.

My Experience

For example, while writing this book I struggled to overcome my self-doubt and my desire to be perfect. I intuitively knew that to connect with you, my reader, I would need to be vulnerable, revealing intimate aspects of my life, and let you know I'm not perfect. Phew—there, I said it. For someone like me who has tried to be the "perfect" son, partner, author and employer, admitting that I have weaknesses is really challenging for me, yet it's also freeing to admit.

I also had to overcome self-doubt since I repeatedly told myself I wasn't a writer. For years I allowed self-doubt to get the best of me, going about my writing in fits and starts and developing an addiction to food along the way. Within twenty minutes of sitting down to write and just when I would start to get on a roll, I felt a virtually indescribable yearning to get up and eat something...*soda crackers*. The first year of writing this book I accomplished very little other than gaining nearly fifteen pounds. After many failed attempts at writing and after eating lots of soda crackers, which I definitely don't recommend (They're not pineal friendly, which I'll talk about in detail later), I became increasingly frustrated and knew I needed to make changes.

After nearly a year, I became fed up with my lackluster results, and I woke up (became conscious) and started doing what I recommend in this book. I reprogrammed my subconscious mind from believing I wasn't good at writing to knowing I am a writer with an important message to share. After a few weeks of repeating affirmations out loud such as, "I am a gifted writer who has insight to share with people who will benefit from reading this book," I changed my experience from being frustrated to really enjoying the process. In order to make the leap from frustration to enjoyment, I had to overcome the impulse to interrupt my writing by eating and to stay in my chair long enough to write.

In summary, to change your experience from frustration or ineffectiveness, to a more desirable and productive outcome, take the following steps:

Gain clarity by thinking consciously about what you desire to experience.

Reprogram your subconscious mind by using positive affirmations spoken out loud and by listening to guided meditations.

Become aware of what you do to stop yourself from achieving your goal.

When you feel the impulse to eat, smoke or drink in order to distract yourself from being present and going deeper within yourself, acknowledge the impulse by saying, "I feel the need to _____ (insert impulse) right now; however, I know by _____ (insert impulse) I won't be able to accomplish my goal as effectively."

Stop yourself from eating, smoking, drinking, or whatever else you do that distracts you from being fully present, even if you have to sit on your hands or phone a friend for support!

Set a crystal clear intention of what you desire to accomplish for the day and allow your subconscious to direct you into making it happen.

Lastly, show up for your day being present, relaxed, and flexible, allowing the universe to work through you rather than you trying to force things to happen.

By repeating these steps daily you will be more productive, happier, joyful and fulfilled all by harnessing the power of your subconscious rather than allowing it to control you.

✳ SELF-ASSESSMENT

◆ Can you think of three things you are grateful for right now and write them in your journal?

◆ In your journal write three affirmations that you can repeat daily while you move your hands in a figure-8 motion.

◆ What can you do each day to be more present?

Chapter 8:
Reconnect Through
the Inner Voyage

"Everyone thinks of changing the world, but no one thinks of changing himself." ~ Leo Tolstoy

How often throughout the day do you take the time to look at yourself in the mirror? Now, I don't mean looking at yourself while you're shaving or brushing your teeth or combing your hair, I'm referring to the times that you stared deeply into your own eyes? If you can't remember the last time you felt a connection with yourself this way, why not take a moment now and go discover what you can find.

I'll wait.

Okay, what did you see? Did you see how beautiful and deep the window to your soul actually is? Getting in touch with your desires and values will help when it comes time to define what true success means for you. The more time you spend in connection with yourself, learning what truly makes you tick, and discovering what elements allow your heart to truly sing, will be invaluable to your journey.

I remember being a child and spending long stretches of time just gazing at my image in the mirror. I looked directly into my own eyes, desiring a reconnection to what I had just left in the spiritual realm. At the time, I was unsure what motivated this soul-searching. What I understand now, as a more developed person that I didn't know back then, was that I could reconnect with the peace, love, and joy I felt in the spiritual realm by forming the reconnection within myself. Our reconnection allows us to once again feel what it is like to be whole and complete. Reconnection can only happen after you let go of egoist pursuits, raise your consciousness, and allow for your spirit to guide you.

The truth is, you're a soul that is timeless and ageless. You have spent far more time in the spiritual realm than you have walking the Earth. The spiritual realm is your true home; it's the place where you have a far greater understanding of your true self. However, each time you leave the spirit realm and reunite your spirit with a body, you experience a process of psychic amnesia. You cannot remember what your mission was before you rejoined the Earth. Your psychic amnesia is, in a way, intentional because if it weren't designed to shield you from all the knowledge you already contain, you would be unable to connect to your life, as you know it. You would spend far more time deciphering the meaning of your past lives, and swimming through thoughts of who you used to be, where you lived and what you did back then. These investigations would dominate this lifetime.

Just contemplate for a moment how much time you spend worrying about your past during *this* lifetime. Some of you might have a strong disbelief in past lives, which is fine, but I invite you to truly explore this thought with me for a moment. Life is so complicated with all that you have to learn, heal and change in order to grow. Do you really believe we only have one try to learn all we need to? Is it possible to get it right in just one try? I'm just giving you this concept as food for thought; allow for independent thinking when it comes to life on Earth. Question ways in which to live it apart from religious beliefs or what friends and family have told you is true.

Be an explorer of your own truth!

So what stands between you and your reconnection to the real you? Fear is the door and ego the doorman.

> *"Named must your fear be before banish it you can."*
> ~ Yoda

What lies at the root of every situation in which we are unable to try, or we feel hindered from producing our best work, from going the distance, from winning the greatest rewards? What learned factor dominates our lives, and prevents us from doing the important work that is laid out before us as a gift from the universe? It is a four-letter word called F-E-A-R.

No human is impervious to fear. My understanding of fear has stemmed from my own experiences, but also from years of coaching clients through their particular obstacles. Having this firsthand interaction with such a wide variety of fears and anxieties has helped me to understand something extremely important: everyone believes that they are alone in their fear. In truth, we are all united because everyone at one time or another experiences fear, and if we recognize this universal truth, we are one step closer to conquering the problem.

Some people believe that fear is a good thing and that it can be wielded as an instrument of change. For instance, fear can keep people alert to potential danger and help our brains generate a response of fight or flight. Others see very little value in taking counsel of their fears as 90% of what is feared never comes to fruition anyway. I believe fears of all kind are best kept to a minimum and need to be managed so that they don't end up managing you!

Breaking Up with Fear

When I was young, fear inhibited me from pursuing certain goals and dreams. I know that this is likely an experience that many readers will relate to. Fear of failure kept me working at jobs that I didn't enjoy for much longer than I should have. My fear of success kept me from experiencing all the joy that comes from opening my heart and giving and receiving love and from reaching my fullest potential. One day it occurred to me, as I was slaving my life away to the machine of work and success, that I would never achieve my goals if I continued to play by other peoples' rules that supposedly kept me "safe." Though the fear of the unknown gripped me completely, I had to break away from the patterns of self-doubt that were dominating my life.

We all have dreams in life that can only be achieved by confronting challenges that may terrify us. Whether it's a huge upheaval of uncertainty, such as starting a completely new career, or moving to a distant country, or something as benign as learning a new sport, it's essential to not only examine why the change scares us, but to face the challenge and do that which scares us most.

In order to live a life of true success and freedom, I had to reevaluate my relationship with the things that made me uncomfortable and confront the things that I feared. Now, when I experience those familiar sensations of trepidation, or if I feel unable to meet a difficult task, I turn myself toward the experience with a deep strength of body and mind, rather than ignoring or avoiding the challenge.

Today, having faced my fears and made changes that have allowed me a level of retrospection, I can detect how fear is playing a part in the lives of my children. I have witnessed fear preventing my capable nine-year-old step-up daughter from learning how to ride a bike. It's painful to see someone you love struggling with an impediment that, if lifted, could bring joy into his or her life. Using patience and understanding, I spoke to her about why she was so afraid. I asked her to consider some questions that I believe are universally helpful in understanding what drives fear at the root of any predicament.

Do you have something that you are afraid to do? Ask yourself the same questions that I asked her:

What's the worst that can happen if you (insert fear here)?

What's the best thing that could happen for you if you (insert fear here)?

Would overcoming (insert fear here) improve the quality of your life?

Finally a question I didn't ask her but my adult readers might find useful: *What's the price you'll have to pay by giving into fear and not pursuing your goals and dreams?*

In order to build a base from which to examine our anxieties, it will be of use to understand what exactly fear is and how to overcome it.

Fear is the creation of ego. Fear is an obstacle that keeps people from living life to the fullest and keeps them living a life beneath what they are truly capable of experiencing. Fear keeps people stuck, unable to evolve or move forward.

Where, you may ask, is the silver lining? The good news about fear is that the experience is truly just an emotion that can be controlled. If you can remember that your fear is just a reaction and merely a symptom, you'll be able to master it and move forward with the important work that you need to do in your life. Taming your fear is possible, and if you can always remember that, you'll go far along your personal journey to attaining true success, enlightenment, passion and joy.

Fear is potent, but it begins to dissipate the more you encounter and experience the things that you're afraid of. When you begin to take steps to confront your fears, you'll notice a lessening of tension in your body and mind. The longer you put off that which scares you, the more difficult it will become to overpower it. Procrastination and avoidance will only add fuel to your fear, but a brave and swift response to the things that scare you will put the power back in your hands.

✳ SELF-ASSESSMENT

Take a moment and think back to a time when you felt fear. Maybe you were afraid to ask your boss for a raise, to ask someone on a date, or to quit your job and start your own business. Did you notice the longer you obsessed over the thing you feared the longer you kept yourself stuck? Did your fears feel larger than life? How did you eventually overcome them? How could you harness that empowerment in the future?

Facing Your Fears Makes Them Disappear

The reality is that 90% of what you fear never comes to fruition. In other words, nine things out of ten that you're currently worried about won't come true anyway. Isn't that an astounding thought? Take a moment and breathe that in. Now, ask yourself, what are you putting off because of fear? Truth is, when you face the very thing you fear, it will literally melt away from your body, mind and spirit. You'll begin to feel the pressure of your fear lifting and you will be able to breathe more easily and take action.

Starting something new is a trigger for fear to rear its ugly head. Making a change in life is another way for fear to creep in. The feeling of uncertainty brings about fear quickly. Not knowing how to do something or what steps to take next can lead you to feeling afraid. If you desire to start your own business or create a line of products but do not have contacts, materials or other resources, you might start feeling afraid. However, there are several ways to combat your fear.

> *Doing that which you fear allows you to move your goals and dreams forward.*

The quickest way to overcome fear is by taking action. The more action you take the lesser your fear will be. The fear of tackling a massive project will not be as overwhelming if you take baby steps every single day. Visit conferences and try to make just one contact. Create a business card or a simple website. The more you expand with small steps, the greater your project will become, and the more your fear will fade away into the background.

Letting go of fear will not only positively impact the success and abundance of your life, but it will also create physical effects that can be detected in the body as well. You may experience better sleep, a more settled stomach, and more energy as you let go of that, which holds you back. If your fears have shown up in your life in the form of an addiction or dependence, you will find those will fade over time. Personal empowerment manifests itself in the body and mind to produce healing effects you may never have imagined were possible.

The Lever Method

You might find it helpful to have some coping mechanisms when it comes to fear. I prefer the "lever" method. I use this the moment I feel fear start to bubble up in my body, which makes my heart pound and my stomach constrict. In my Wealth Mastery Workshops™ I teach a few simple techniques to assist my clients to overcome fear.

The first technique is called "the lever." This works best if used the moment you start to feel afraid. Close your eyes and bring to mind an image of a large lever, which represents the fear you are feeling. You'll notice that the lever is in the upright position, which indicates your fear is "on." Now, see yourself standing near the lever. Wrap your hand around it and take a deep breath. As you exhale, hammer down the lever, while saying, "Fear be gone!" Finally, allow feelings of confidence and faith to come forward, and see how much better you feel.

> *Do something to take hold of fear*
> *and not let fear take hold of you!*

Seminar attendees have also shared other ways to eliminate fear, such as putting whatever they are afraid of in a bubble and watching it float away. Some simply watch, as their fear becomes a cute little puppy that they train, rather than letting the puppy run the show. Perhaps you'll come up with your own way. Whatever works for you is great.

I have many other techniques to eliminate fear and you can find those on my website. One helpful way is to break up with fear by writing fear a "Dear John" letter. For the actual wording of the letter go to: www.thewealthquest.com/bookresources where you can find the letter on breaking up with fear and moving in with faith! After you write your breakup letter with fear, create a ceremony and burn the letter. Burning the letter allows for the energy to transmute and change and for you to no longer have to feel afraid.

Feeling Overwhelmed Is Just a State of Mind

A derivative of fear—although not as detrimental to your success and way easier to manage—is feeling overwhelmed. The key to managing feeling overwhelmed is to divert the feeling as soon as you realize that it's taking over. For example, let's say that while sitting and working at your desk, you glance around and see endless stacks of papers. All of the projects that you have to do are putting pressure on your mind, and your heart begins to pound. Your head fills with unproductive thoughts such as, "I'll never get anything done," or "Where do I even start?"

If you find yourself incredibly overwhelmed and unsure what to do first, there are a variety of methods you can employ to alleviate the stress of the situation and get your mission back on track. Rather than choosing to avoid the situation—for example, by leaving your desk—stop yourself and take a deep breath.

Once you have treated yourself to a nice big breath, begin to offer yourself positive affirmations that will shut down your fight or flight response and return you to a level of equilibrium. Remind yourself that these feelings are normal by saying inwardly, "Everything is okay. I'm only feeling overwhelmed. I can handle this." The simple act of acknowledging your feelings to yourself will free you to take action and make steps toward something productive rather than remaining stuck and overwhelmed.

Next, write a simple to-do list of easy tasks that can be done relatively quickly.

After that, get to work right away, striking items off the list and adding new ones as the day progresses. Making a list and ticking off all the things that you have accomplished, even if they are things that you do every day, will give you a sense of feeling productive and will help displace your previous feelings.

The best time to make a to-do list is at night before leaving your office or before going to sleep. This way you'll sleep better and can start the next day feeling more capable and organized.

While you're working, don't allow other people to distract you. Here's a trick that I used successfully when I worked in corporate America. I always made sure the chairs in my office were piled high with stacks of papers to discourage coworkers from sitting in my office if they dropped by. The piles were so enormous that it would require a lot of effort to move them. Still to this day, even though I work from home, the only chair in my office (I sit on an exercise ball) is piled high with papers.

You can develop your own tricks for gaining the solitude you need.

When you're able to recognize what is causing you to feel overwhelmed, stop yourself, take a deep breath and remind yourself you're just feeling overwhelmed and you're in charge of the situation.

Another way that I combat feeling overwhelmed is to start my day by doing things that help me feel balanced and grounded.

In as little as five minutes you can set the intention for your day while stretching and breathing. Doing so will help you be more productive, flexible and focused. Flexibility is key to keeping your body fit and to maintain healthy joints. Stretching doesn't need to be overly difficult, nor do you need a large space. In fact, going outside in the morning and walking through the grass barefoot will help you connect with the Earth's energies and ground you. Being grounded allows you to breathe more easily and be more flexible and relaxed, all of which are ideal conditions for you to set clear intentions for what you want to accomplish during the day.

For those who live in big cities and don't have access to parks or a grassy area, or if it's winter and going outside isn't ideal, try placing a towel on the floor near a window. Listen to peaceful music, close your eyes and visualize being out in nature, connecting to the Earth and her energies. As the saying goes, where there's a will there's a way, so find a way each day to connect with yourself and to the Earth. Creating a regular routine of breathing and stretching will help you start your day being centered and balanced, both of which are essential to eliminate feeling overwhelmed and for you to have an amazing day.

✳ SELF-ASSESSMENT

◆ What is your deepest dream or lofty goal?

◆ What keeps you from attaining either one?

◆ What steps can you take today toward achieving your goal or making your dream come true? If there are many steps, think about them in detail and write them down.

◆ Do you need the help of friends, family or a mentor?

Chapter 9:
Harness the Power of Your
Mind

*"Minds are like flowers, they only open when the
time is right."* ~ Stephen Richards

From my meditation room overlooking Tampa Bay, I see pastel shades of pink, blue and purple dancing across the horizon, ushering in a new day. I start my day the same most mornings, sitting in meditation while giving thanks for all that comes into my life. However, this particular morning was different. While meditating, I notice out of the corner of my eye Perry, the local resident pelican as he begins his quest for his morning meal. The lifespan of pelicans is relatively short. This isn't surprising, given that their food source can be obtained only by diving headfirst into the water at a high speed. Still, despite the difficulty of their hunting habits, the challenging act is never a sure success. Thankfully we human beings do not have to dive into deep and dark water in order to obtain our precious sustenance. If our quest for nourishment were equally difficult, I have a feeling that many among us might go hungry.

I watch as Perry tirelessly repeats the same pattern. He seems completely unfocused in the early morning hours, lazily diving off his 20-foot perch, and repeatedly missing his mark. I shake my head and think to myself, "That sure looks like a lot of wasted effort." However, as the morning progresses, and after countless failed attempts, Perry's behavior takes on the tenets of innovation. He appears more determined and focused than he was when he began his search. He takes his time gazing steadily into the water and readies himself for his dive by rocking his body from side to side. Now, intensely focused and with lightning speed, Perry leaves his 20-foot perch. Seconds later he rises victoriously from the water, stretching his long neck upwards and swallowing his breakfast whole.

Success! How sweet it is!

After witnessing this scene unfold each morning for weeks, I began to wonder why Perry was only successful after his initial failure. It's only after numerous attempts that he finally becomes focused and determined and is able to successfully pursue his goal with passion.

Clearly, Perry already possesses the skill that allows him to be successful day after day, so why doesn't he employ those skills first rather than wait until after he has missed his mark time and time again? While growing up, did Perry see his parents do the same? Maybe he learned his way of fishing by watching his companions. Who knows, maybe Perry went to fishing school and was taught, fishing is "hard work" or, worse yet, that "there aren't enough fish in the sea."

I have found in my coaching practice that people tend to make their quest for success as difficult as Perry's pursuit of breakfast. Many work very hard because they have been told that it's the only way to success. However, working hard is not the only path to success, nor does it guarantee that you'll be successful. Bring into your mind a visual of those people who work really hard: ditch diggers, laborers, tradesmen all come to mind for me.

Are all those hard working people experiencing success in their lives?

No.

The belief that you have to work hard to become successful is actually false and exhausting. There is much more to the success equation than just working hard. In fact, some people find that when they combine working hard with working smart, their chances of success rise dramatically. These are people who might have taken a risk and started their own business, still working hard all the while, yet now they are working for themselves and building something of value rather than just trading time for money. Still others, though, find that working smart and listening to and following their gut feelings elevates them to an entirely new level of success.

Keep the End in Mind When You Begin

What is an essential ingredient for you to experience true success? You need to have an idea of where you want to go in life and what you desire to accomplish. Not sure where or what that is? Answer the following questions and you just might get a glimpse into where you are headed.

What do you truly desire?
What really, really, really makes your heart sing?
What are you doing when time seems to fly by?

Maybe you're reading this and thinking to yourself, "I still have no idea what makes my heart sing or what's next for me." If you feel unanchored and unsure of what your life needs to truly make it amazing, it's ok. As you progress along your journey of self-knowing, you'll begin to naturally turn in the direction of that which you desire. New opportunities that resonate with you will begin to present themselves- and a feeling of wellbeing and joy are clues that you're headed in the right direction.

Similar to the long jumper flying through the air with outstretched limbs, he is clear about where he wants to land. Successful golfers visualize where they want their ball to go before they hit it. Your job is to know where you want to go in life and what you want to experience, and then harness the power of your mind via your thoughts to get you there.

Inspired Thoughts From the Universe

> *"Whether you think you can or can't, you're right."*
> ~ Henry Ford

Everything and anything you see, feel, hold or touch started as an idea or thought in someone's mind. Throughout the course of any given day you'll have anywhere from 50,000 to 80,000 thoughts fluttering around in your mind. Think about that for a moment—that means on average you have 48 thoughts per minute. A lot of these thoughts are just fleeting, are mostly processed and stored by your subconscious mind, and don't go anywhere or lead to anything.

For instance, let's say you're walking down the road and your mind is processing quick thoughts about the weather, the person you just passed, projects you're working on, your relationship, how comfortable your shoes are, where your keys are, or what you said to your friend earlier that day. Suffice it to say, your mind is always busy and in that busyness some very important ideas and thoughts can get lost or are left unacknowledged. These are your inspired thoughts that are literally dropped in from the universe. It's these thoughts from the universe that are the important ones to notice. They hold the solutions to your current challenges and offer inspiration for things such as starting a new business or expanding your current one. Learning to identify these thoughts will be one of your biggest challenges since they are subtle, they come in the form of your own voice, and they come without warning and leave quickly.

These thoughts generally come when your conscious thinking mind is occupied. That's why people who do walking meditations receive so much valuable information because the conscious thinking mind (ego) is occupied by walking, which frees up the higher conscious mind to deliver useful information. You don't have to learn to meditate in order to receive this information; in fact lots of amazing insights can come to you as you go about your day. For example, washing dishes, showering, brushing your teeth, gardening, walking, or reading a book is prime time for inspired thoughts to visit. Your job is to invite that visiting thought in to stay a while and see if it's a good fit for you.

I have learned that when I jog on my treadmill amazing ideas, inspiration and insights come to me so often that I have a handheld recording device so that when the ideas start flowing in I can record them and use the information later for my courses or books.

When it comes to your thoughts, your job is to identify and distinguish between limiting thoughts of the ego and empowering thoughts brought to you via your higher self (soul). Remember that thoughts that are either limiting or comparative come via ego, while thoughts or ideas that assist you in being more productive, joyful, creative, or loving come from your higher self. A quick way to discover the source (ego or soul) of your thought is by asking yourself does having this thought prompt me to compare or relate? Thoughts that allow you to relate better to yourself or others are those that when explored further will transform your life.

Thoughts are the instrument that modern-day alchemists use to transform the invisible to visible.

What you think of most often grows and becomes your reality. When you combine your inspired thoughts with the other tools in this book, you'll soon have the experience of abundance in everything from health to automatic wealth.

Remember, when it comes to your thoughts your job is to:

1) Become aware of the source. Is it ego or your higher self?

2) Acknowledge the thoughts from your higher self. Remember, inspired thoughts are fleeting so record them right away.

3) Take action when you feel inspired.

4) Ask the universe for more guidance.

5) When you feel guided, take action.

6) Be grateful.

It's that simple—try not to complicate it by over thinking.

The Power from Saying "I Am...."

"I am" statements are the most powerful statements you can make. When you say, "I am _____," you put the universe and others on notice as to how to treat you, how to respond to you, and how to relate to you. When Donald Trump was a young boy, his sisters referred to him as "The Great I Am," because he communicated his desires clearly and continues to do so. "I am" statements bring you right into the present, which is the only place from which you can manifest success in life.

Muhammad Ali demonstrated that he knew the power of "I am" statements when he said, "'I am the greatest!' I said that even before I knew I was," and he certainly manifested being one of the greatest boxers of all time.

What you say about yourself speaks volumes. It's important that you always speak kindly of yourself, without judgment. By communicating the words "I am _____," you're aligning your inner belief and your thoughts with what is truly attainable for you regardless of your current situation.

Does this take some practice? Yes, and the great thing is as you experiment with these techniques you'll quickly receive feedback based on what you manifest (or don't), which will allow you to adjust by doing more of what works and leave behind what doesn't. The following story is true and exemplifies the power of thought, belief, prayer, visualization, and acting as if. Enjoy.

Act As If

While growing up, Cynthia Stafford's mother instilled in her a habit of positive thinking and meditation, and championed the importance of giving back to others as an important part of daily life. Cynthia is a naturally generous person who grew up loving the arts. Even as a youth, by sharing from her allowance she often donated money to various causes in order to support her community and be a part of change in the world.

Despite the promising groundwork provided to her by her family and experiences in her early years, Cynthia's adulthood was unfortunately filled with heartache and unfulfilled dreams.

Cynthia found herself struggling to make ends meet. Despite how hard she worked she was trapped in a situation where her bills consistently exceeded her paycheck.

Cynthia then experienced a life-altering personal tragedy when her brother was killed in a sudden accident while crossing the street.

Cynthia was single, financially unstable and broken hearted by the death of her brother; however, she was not disheartened. When her brother's children were suddenly left parentless, she couldn't ignore the feeling deep within her heart to take them in and look after them the best she could, despite the already difficult conditions of her life. Unfortunately, soon after offering her home to the children, Cynthia was pressured by the court system to break up her brother's five children, and she was urged to place them in foster homes. Cynthia knew deep within splitting up her nieces and nephews wasn't an option, and she desperately hoped to keep the family united by any means possible.

One day, as she was going about her normal routine the dollar amount $112,000,000 popped into her head. Cynthia knew this was a sign from the universe so she wrote the number down on a piece of paper and put it under her pillow. Then she began to "act as if" she had already received the money by interviewing several financial planners and looking at million dollar homes that were for sale. Soon after putting the number $112,000,000 under her pillow, Cynthia noticed that the California lottery jackpot had reached $112,000,000. Upon meditating she knew the jackpot was a sign from the universe, so she bought a $2.00 ticket.

Lo and behold, she won the entire jackpot! Suddenly her fate and the lives of her loved ones had changed forever.

After winning the Mega Millions lottery she said, "Everyone was shocked but me. I had already begun checking out financial advisors." Cynthia's story is a perfect example of "acting as if," because she didn't let her zero bank account balance steal her dream of keeping her nieces and nephews together. Cynthia knew that she would have millions of dollars to invest, and now she lives the life that she dreamed into being.

All the elements were present in order for Cynthia's desire to manifest. She had a vision larger than herself, which was to keep her brother's children together and to do anything that she could not to have to break them apart. She received an inspired thought from the universe and she wrote it down, helping to make it tangible and real. She then allowed the universe to guide her as to which step to take next. It's important to note that she didn't worry or fret about how she was going to get $112,000,000 she simply trusted and began to "act as if." Cynthia may have had the only winning ticket for the California lottery that day however, her generous spirit shown through when Cynthia split her winnings with her one remaining sibling, a brother and her father. Cynthia truly is an ambassador of acting as if, and her story is a wonderful example of the rewards that can come from taking action after receiving inspired thought.

The moral of the story is simple: no matter how things look right now, stay true to your vision. Keep an open heart, have unshakeable faith, take inspired action, and never give up on your dreams.

✳ SELF-ASSESSMENT

- ◆ Pretend that today is your birthday. This year, you have decided to give yourself a special gift. It's the gift of always finding the easy, simple and divine path. How would your life change with such a gift?

- ◆ Fill in the blank, I AM _____. Keep affirming this statement over and over until you see your desires and dreams manifest. Your "I AM _____ statement works best when spoken out loud either to others or to yourself as you focus your eyes on your thumbs and move your hands in a figure-8 pattern.

> *"All the powers in the universe are already ours. It is we who have put our hands before our eyes and cry that it is dark."* ~ Swami Vivekananda

Chapter 10:
Setting Intentions Gets the
Universe's Attention

"All the breaks you need in life wait within your imagination. Imagination is the workshop of your mind, capable of turning mind energy into accomplishment and wealth." ~ Napoleon Hill

Setting your intentions with the universe is very similar to using a search engine on a computer. Your intentions are sent out to the universe, and in return people, places and things come to you. The more specific the input, the better your chances are of receiving those things aligned with your input. Clarity is key; being specific and crystal clear about what you desire will produce favorable results, whereas vagueness will stop the manifesting process from taking a successful hold on your life. Being specific about what you're intending is as important as being open to something even greater happening for you. For example, the year I turned forty I decided it was time for me to learn how to cook. I enrolled in a cooking class taught by a local chef who was trained at Le Cordon Bleu Cooking Academy (yes, it was the same one Julia Child attended). At that time, I had never heard of Le Cordon Bleu so I did not understand the level of prestige that was attached to the name. My French was also quite rusty, so I mistakenly thought it was a cooking school that mostly dealt with blue cheese and chicken, both of which I liked (at the time). However, after the fourth class of flambéing, sautéing and flambéing a sauté, the instructor looked over at me and said, "Jaden, this is your fourth class. Tell me what have you learned so far." With a glazed look in my eye, and without skipping a beat, I said, "Nancy, I have learned to really appreciate when someone cooks me dinner!" It may not have been the answer she wanted to hear; however, it was an insight that I myself truly needed to gain from that experience!

Staying open to all outcomes (regardless of your original intention) allows for even greater experiences than you ever thought possible and ensures your highest and best interests will always be met.

Inspiration Without Perspiration

When your intentions are aligned with inspiration from the universe, prepare yourself for wonderful things, because that is a sign that success is on its way! Recently I read a biography of J.K. Rowling, author of the Harry Potter series. According to the biography, J.K. started working on the Harry Potter sequence in 1990, when "the idea ... simply fell into my head."

Inspired thoughts, when acted upon, can truly impact and spectacularly change your life for the better! Tune your mind to acknowledge those thoughts that come to you repeatedly, because they are almost certainly trying to tell you something. Those are the thoughts that speak to you so loudly you can't ignore them.

Inspired thoughts are another way the universe gets your attention. Inspiration from the universe may come in many forms, including in the form of dreams experienced during both day and night, through the power of music, encounters with nature and art, the plot line of a fascinating book or film, or even from valuable conversations that you have with your friends and loved ones. Really, it could come in the form of any activity in which you set your conscious, thinking mind aside and allow ideas to flow through you.

I and many of my students have received valuable information while individually carrying out simple acts such as: reading, listening to music, exercising, gardening, painting, sculpting, watching TV, walking on the beach and, of course, during the all-important act of relaxing!

During my travels, I had the pleasure of meeting Thomas Bähler, a world-renowned musician turned author, who has worked closely with Quincy Jones, Steven Spielberg, and Elvis Presley. Thomas shared an amazing story with me regarding what his father, Jack, told him about having ideas and being creative. The story inspired me and resonated deeply within me, and I wanted to share it with you.

Here's the story exactly how Thomas told it to me:

When I was six years old I asked my father, "How do I be creative?"

"I'll tell you how I do it," my father replied. "I declare what I want, and then I let it go." And I'm six years old, so I'm like, "Huh?"

And he said, "Well, son, when you declare something, you send energy out. And it will come back to you if it serves others as well."

Now I'm starting to get it.

He said, "And once you declare, you let it go, but you remain very vigilant because it will come to you. But when it comes to you, you may not recognize it at first because if you did, it wouldn't be new. And then, you would invite that idea in whatever format comes into you. Invite that idea into you. And you take care of it like you would a neighbor who came over to visit you.

You get it a glass of water. You cling to it. And if that idea is supposed to stay with you, it will become part of you. And if it is not supposed to stay with you, and it's just there for a visit, it will go tell other ideas its found a good host. And it has been what I lived my life by and its given me so much peace."

"I believe we all are channels for the universe to work through," said Thomas. "Quincy Jones and I are very different.

We were business partners. He is also my son's Godfather. So, we're very close. He and I have stayed up all night, many nights talking about this very concept. And we call it the muse. And we actually both think of her as a woman. And we love the muse, and you have to gain access to the muse. We gain access to the muse by focusing on what we want, by also learning about what it is that we want. Once we know what we want, we were curious about it. We say, how do they do that? How did that happen? I wonder how it is. All of a sudden, now we're students but we don't know we're students."

Thomas further said regarding his muse, "I call her angel. She comes to me in a form of energy that is sort of copper color."

Thomas candidly shared with me he got a job with Ford Motor Company that allowed him to make a "ton of money." Soon the gig was over and he said, "I thought to myself, I like that income stream. How do I maintain that? So I asked the question. That was everything dad used to say—ask the question. He asked the universe, 'How do I maintain this lifestyle?' And then, it came to me as a song. And I felt; well, I've never written a song. But I did. And so, when the song came to me, I sat down at the piano. My job was to realize it. That song had come to me for me to bring it to the world. And that's my service. So I wrote the song and got on a plane and went to ski with my buddies in Europe. And I gave it to my brother to bring to the producer. And I said, 'By the way, if he doesn't like it, *you* wrote it.' Well,

I got a call from him while I'm in Austria. And he says, 'you got Bobby Sherman's next single.'"

That was Thomas's experience. He easily manifested a life of abundance from listening to his muse and following her guidance.

Not everyone has such an easy and joyful experience. In fact, many people erroneously believe that the universe has an agenda (that it wants something from them) other than what they want for themselves. The universe doesn't work that way. A little thing called free will allows you to decide what you want to be, do, or have, always and in all ways.

Everyone has complete freedom when it comes to his or her thoughts. During the course of the day you're inundated with thousands of thoughts vying for your attention. The thoughts aligned with your desires are the ones needing most attention. Your job is to figure out exactly what you want to experience in all situations in life. Furthermore, if you don't enjoy something you're experiencing then change it, you always have the power to do so at anytime no matter what! Knowing you can change your situation at anytime regardless of whom or what is involved should give you peace of mind and faith in the way the universe works.

Rest assured that the universe is working for you, to assist you in receiving what your heart desires. At times, you might not be aware of what your heart desires, which is perfectly natural. Not everyone knows at a young age what he or she wants to be when they grow up, and some take longer than others to figure it out. What you can be sure of, though, is that the universe does not have an agenda different than what you intend for yourself. You're in charge of what you choose to experience and what you accomplish on Earth is not random.

For some, this knowledge is a huge pill to swallow. For others—those who are willing to experience their lives awake and aware—this fact will come as no surprise. However, many people do not trust in their ability to follow their inner guidance. So many implore the universe to give them a "sign" as to the direction they need to go, and preferably a large billboard dropping from the sky with an arrow showing them the way.

The universe gives direction in subtle ways, and you must be alert to its signals. Examples of these clues are: subtle thoughts that come and go quickly. Events that at the time seemed "random" yet in hindsight made perfect sense. A chance encounter with someone where you received advice that was exactly what you needed to hear. A distinctly clear inner knowing or feeling that led you to take certain action or to go in a certain direction.

Acting upon the signs you receive will bring you more signs and clues along your path. Another benefit that comes from living life consciously is that you won't need the proverbial two-by-four smack in order to receive the message from the universe. *The way of the universe is gentle and graceful. If you need reminding, just take a walk in nature and look for the balance*

and calm that exists. The creator of the universe is your creator, and all of its power, peace and perfection are available to you.

> *You don't have to wait for the universe to meet you halfway; the universe is always fully present and is waiting for you!*

One of the most beneficial things you can do for yourself after you acknowledge receiving inspiration from the universe is to take action! The action I am referring to is inspired action. The difference between inspired and non-inspired action is that inspired action leads to productivity and never requires you to "stay busy." Being busy is not always productive; being busy can often lead to ineffectiveness, as your mind gets cluttered with unnecessary information and tasks. Try replacing the need to be busy with the desire to be productive, and recognize the innumerable ways in which that simple shift of perspective can change your day. Focusing on being productive will allow you to breathe more easily, freeing your mind to receive inspiration from your partner, the universe (more on this later).

✳ SELF-ASSESSMENT

♦ Where do you feel most relaxed, and most inspired?

♦ What unconventional methods have brought you your most brilliant thoughts?

♦ How do you listen to your inner voice?

Success Through Intentions

Now it's your turn. You have come to the part in this book where you now have a chance to get clear about what you intend for your life. Perhaps you desire to work less and enjoy your life more, or you desire to have financial freedom so that you can travel around the world with your family, or maybe your heart is telling you to quit your job and start a business. Whatever your heart desires, you can have it all. It doesn't matter how educated or uneducated you are, what background you come from, what gender you are, or what economic class you're in. Nor does it matter how much money you have in your bank account.

What matters most deeply is your desire for change! What matters is your willingness to do things differently than you have in the past. And as for timing, the best moment to begin this important change is right now. The time has come for you to remember the dreams you once had! Not the petty day-to-day desires that drive you, but rather the big and lasting dreams that underpin your life. The dreams that leave you breathless with excitement, the dreams that fill you up with passion and make your heart sing.

This is your journal time.

Take a moment and close your eyes, allow yourself to feel centered and connected to the universe. Breathe deeply and allow for a feeling of gratitude to come to you. When you are smiling from within and are filled with gratitude open your eyes and start writing an answer to these questions:

What do I desire?

What would I do if money were no object?

What changes would I like to make in my life starting now?

These three simple questions could start you on a path toward a more fulfilling and joyful life. Trust your instincts and answer the questions without hesitating. By taking the time to get clear about what you intend for your life the universe can now start to line up the "how" part for your intentions to manifest.

The Whiteboard Brings Results!

Our vast and diverse experiences are what make life worth living. We all, at one time or another, have had the experience of heartache, joy, love, passion, fulfillment, happiness, success, failure, travel, work, and the list goes on and on.

The process of manifesting begins after we decide what we desire to experience. Having techniques available to us to help shorten the learning curve are always helpful. A particular technique that works well is what I refer to in my workshops as, the whiteboard technique. When I'm working on manifesting something or someone into my life, first I focus my thoughts on what I desire to experience. I do this by asking myself:

"What do I desire to experience from manifesting _____?"

Next, I create a *mental picture* of what I desire to manifest. I place my mental picture on a whiteboard in the upper left corner of my mind and I leave it there for an undetermined amount of days or weeks. This is an imaginary whiteboard, and I feel it near the left frontal lobe of my brain. I also have a physical whiteboard in my office, but I have a tendency to over clutter that board with too many ideas. The imaginary whiteboard for some reason always remains free of clutter, holding only one idea at a time.

Next, while relaxing or meditating I edit and refine my idea, returning to assess my desires while also holding the vision of what I want to manifest in the forefront of my mind or in my thoughts.

Finally, I take action, but only after receiving inspired thoughts, visions or gut feelings.

For example, recently I set a clear intention to create and produce a card deck that people could consult if they had questions regarding their life and needed answers. My original thought was, "I desire to create a card deck that could help people make decisions easily regarding their personal and professional lives." Then I waited for an "inspired thought." The thought that quickly arrived was: "The deck will have 44 cards." This made sense, since 4 + 4 = 8, which is the traditional number signifying abundance. In my mind's eye, I envisioned the 44-card deck and put the words, "44-card deck" on my "imaginary whiteboard" to work with and refine.

To keep each intention separate and clear in my mind, I create a new whiteboard for each vision that I seek to manifest. I have no more than three whiteboards operating simultaneously, so that I can keep all of my aspirations clearly organized in my mind. You will know when an idea or concept is worthy enough to make its way onto your whiteboard because it will be something you're really passionate about. Why the whiteboard? Because it keeps your really important goals in the forefront of your mind while you take time to edit and refine your vision. Whenever inspired thoughts drop in, add those to your board. Also, simultaneously write down on paper the same intention you placed on your whiteboard. Committing your vision and all the ideas you have on paper will help your vision materialize. When you write a goal or vision down you are adding more "weight" to your goal, thus letting the universe know you are quite sincere about your vision or goal materializing.

Co-Creating With the Universe

Hopefully at this point you are beginning to grasp that you are not solely responsible for making things happen in your life. In fact, the truth is, you are connected to the universe and to its creator, and you are co-creating your life with the divine in every moment.

That statement should set your mind at ease so you can trust that the universe has your back especially when it comes to you manifesting your heart's desires. That being said, another important key to manifesting is, after you're clear about your heart's desire, *let it go....*

What this means is that you don't have to stress and strain to figure out *how* something is going to come about. Trust that you have done your homework by first, figuring out what you desire, then setting your crystal-clear intention. After that, all you have to do is wait to see what comes into your life. I call this phenomenon "drop in your lap," because whatever you are truly meant to be, do, or have will come to you and it will be so obvious you can't miss it. Your job is simply to remain open and conscious, and to not clutter your mind, so that new ideas can have room to drop in.

Pause and breathe that in for a moment.

From an outsider's perspective, it might have appeared as though I was doing nothing in order to achieve my desire to create a card deck. However, I knew better. I had set a crystal-clear intention and I trusted in the universe to bring clues as to what action was needed and guide me toward the success that I sought.

Sure enough, three weeks later, as I was relaxing at home, I became inspired, and I began to write. Before I knew it, the card deck sprung to life and all forty-four cards poured onto the pages in front of me. This included elaborate and exciting details, such as the names and brief descriptions for each particular card. I was amazed by how easily and relatively quickly the cards manifested themselves once I had opened myself to their message.

Within a few weeks after the cards appeared to me, I was on a path to complete my mission and I was led to the right people to assist me in anchoring my vision into reality.

The universe helped guide me to my goal, but it was up to me to recognize true inspiration and to navigate my way through the process. Keeping the image of a completed card deck on my whiteboard was my role in the creating process. The universe's role was to lead me in the right direction to develop every aspect of the deck. The universe was clear and direct with me by always dropping in thoughts that led me to the right people and places for the cards to manifest in physical form. My conscious thinking mind wavered with the idea of putting a different image on each card, similar to other card decks, yet I felt strongly in my gut that my deck was going to be different than the others already on the market. Soon, the idea of having separate images for each card was replaced with the idea of having "action steps"

that corresponded with the particular wealth and wisdom concept for each card.

The next step came in naming the cards. I ran several ideas by a dear friend, Hailey Wiseman, who is a beautiful person teaching online workshops in healing and self-development. Hailey shared with me that she really liked the words "Wealth & Wisdom," so I ran with her contribution.

It can be extremely valuable to share your dreams with someone you know who will assist you on your path. Notice I didn't say that you should share your ideas with everyone, as some people will dissuade you from pursuing your goals based on their own fear.

The last task was finding the right graphic designer to create an image for the cards that was similar to the image I was seeing in my mind. One night, while surfing the web, I came across a logo that caught my eye. After further exploration, I discovered that the person who created the logo did so by winning a contest from an online logo contest site. My inner voice told me that posting a contest would be an excellent way to see a wide selection of art and make a wise decision to best represent my message. I posted a contest giving crystal-clear instructions for the artists as to the image I desired for my cards. Within a few short days an artist perfectly captured my vision, and I knew I had the winner.

The image for the front of the cards was now complete. However, the backside of the card—the side that had the description and action steps—was bland in appearance and generally unexciting to look at. I encouraged the person handling my card layout to try different color borders for the cards in an effort to make the white background and black font look less stark, yet nothing felt quite right. I continued to stay open, and trusted that the universe would bring me something to make the back of the cards complete.

> *Always keep moving in the direction of your dreams and goals, knowing for certain you will receive helpful information at the right time.*

Another necessary step to having your dreams take hold and your visions manifest is to always trust in the universe's ability to deliver the goods and to show you what steps to take. Remember, "trust" is a verb, not a noun.

This step is where a lot of people get tripped up, they take a few steps toward achieving their goals, however, if their goals don't materialize as fast as they would like, they stop taking action and abandon their dream.

If you give up on your dream so will the universe! Staying committed to your dream will allow the universe to stay committed to it also.

I trusted and believed in my vision and I wasn't at all put off by not figuring out a solution for the back of the cards. In fact the day I was scheduled to email the PDF files to the printer, I still hadn't found a solution for the back of the cards. That morning, I was taking a shower (which is how I get a lot of my good ideas) and while thinking about the card deck, an image of a scroll appeared in my mind. "That's it!" I screamed. I knew the scroll that I was seeing in my mind should be used as a backdrop for the text, further reinforcing the theme of wisdom that I had hoped to share.

Knowing the image, text and design were complete; I still felt like I needed another sign that moving forward with initially producing 1,000 card decks was in alignment with my soul's purpose, so I asked the universe for a sign. Standing in my kitchen, which is just off of the garage, I invited the universe to send me a signal indicating that I should go ahead with printing the cards. Within seconds, I heard the mechanical garage door open automatically, which it had never done on its own before! Laughing, I knew the universe was telling me the cards would open many doors.

Vision Boards Work if You Work Them

Ever since the movie *The Secret* was popularized, there has been a lot of discussion whether or not vision boards are useful. Personally, I think they can be useful and even powerful if done correctly. Plus they are a terrific way to introduce anyone (even kids) to the concepts of goal setting, creative visualization and to manifesting principles.

Creating a vision board is simple. First, you will need something for the backing such as construction paper, cardboard, or corkboard to glue, clip or pin pictures and words onto. Vision boards work similarly to whiteboards in that you must first be clear about what you would like to manifest. Next, find pictures or phrases that best represent your vision, and paste them onto your board.

Keep this powerful tool in a place where you can see it every day. Investing at least ten minutes a day by connecting with the images is key to seeing them manifest in your life. You do this by connecting with your heart and feelings as you visualize yourself having already manifested that which you desire. For example, if you desire to live on the water, clip out a picture of the type of home you would like to live in, including the type of water you desire to see when you look out your windows and put it on your board. If you desire to live on the ocean be clear about which ocean and where. If you desire to live in a home overlooking a lake then find a picture of a home on a lake. I think you get the idea.

Next, invest approximately ten minutes a day looking at the picture of the home and envision yourself living in a home with a similar water view. While envisioning yourself living in the home, use all of your senses to conjure up feelings and allow them to flow through your body. What will it feel like to dip your toe in the water, or to breathe in the fresh or salt-water air?

Incorporating multiple senses helps anchor your vision into reality.

Your brain is designed to solve problems and it can't tell the difference between what is real and what is imagined. So as you live in your current house and spend time each day imagining yourself living in another home on the water, your brain will work on bringing you opportunities that will allow the waterfront home to materialize. Frequent strong feelings of gratitude for having already received your desire (even if you haven't) influence the speed at which your desires manifest. You might find the more time you invest in this exercise each day the quicker your vision will manifest. In my life, the steps I need to take for my vision to unfold simply "pop into my head" during the course of my day. I think you will find this too, when you allow yourself to visualize your heart's desires and believe you are worthy of that desire you will be guided to take action.

Guidance, when acted upon allows for your vision to materialize.

Once your vision has manifested give thanks and gratitude to the universe for bringing you what you sought.

Your "work" in having your vision unfold, is for you to figure out what your vision of success (or anything else) looks like. Remember the long jumper? He or she is only focused on how far to jump, not with what happens between the time of push off and landing.

Being dogmatic about your vision taking physical form is of equal importance, as is letting go of the desire to make something happen. When you try to force things to happen, you're not allowing for the gentle and graceful way of the universe to make things happen for you. Relax and allow the universe to line things up with your vision, and in time it will be revealed in physical form. You can always refine and edit your vision until it feels right to you, and remain open to ideas or suggestions from others. However, always go with what resonates with you.

When you consciously set your intentions in order to get the universe's attention, you will begin to receive inspired ideas on a more regular basis. You will become attuned to this method of reception, and the right ideas for you will feel different than other ideas and this will help you know which to act on. Conversely, if something is unfolding in a way that feels forced, that is a sign that you're leaving the universe's assistance on the table. When you feel a sense of struggle taking hold within you, know that is ego trying to get you to fit a square peg in a round hole, which never works.

Remember:

♦ Give yourself a gift and give up having to struggle.

♦ Move in a direction that feels right to you.

♦ Only follow the path that you are being guided to follow.

♦ Seek and take hold of the inspiration that is being offered to you by the universe.

◆   Utilize your tools to realize your vision.

Applying these strategies will allow you to move in the direction of your dreams deliberately and with confidence, which will give you the motivation to continue taking action! Your continued action will eventually allow you to see your heart's desires manifest in tangible form.

✳ SELF-ASSESSMENT

◆   Take a few deep breaths, relax with this exercise, and allow your mind to expand and get out of your comfort zone. The more uncomfortable you feel with the "largeness" of this intention, the greater your potential for success. Ready?

◆   Open your journal and document your response to the following questions (take your time here):

"What would I attempt to be, do, or have if I were guaranteed to succeed?"

Next, *"Is this in alignment with my definition of true success?"*

I have asked and answered these questions countless times in my life and have found my answers change as I mature and grow. As you evolve spiritually and emotionally, your answers will change too, how could they not? What you once deemed important—let's say, when you were younger—might hold little significance for you today. That's why it's fun to write down your answers and in time look back and see how much you have matured and grown.

Part II

Revitalize Your Vessel: *Body*

Chapter 11:
How to Activate Your
Magnetic Center: Your
Brain's Core

"Imagination is the eye of the soul."
~ Joseph Joubert, *Pensées*

Intuitively, I've sensed and felt that we are all connected not only to each other, but also to everything on the planet and in the universe. Furthermore, I have always had an innate understanding that we are but walking magnets, possessing the ability to attract whatever it is we choose to experience regardless of our situation. However, this knowingness wasn't enough for me, I also wanted to know "how" the process of magnetizing our heart's desires works.

The seemingly simple, three letter question, "How?" took me on an incredible journey that lasted years and culminated in the realization of how the mind, body and spirit connection works and where it takes place.

There is a specific place within each of us where we connect to source and where we magnetize experiences and manifest our true desires. It's a magnificent place in our bodies that has crystals; hundreds to be exact, and these crystals create a ripe environment for us to connect with others via our thoughts. Crystals act as a conductor and transmitter, sending and receiving messages with other people and with those in the spiritual realm. Incredible as it may sound, that is how you're physically wired. You are perfectly designed to connect with others in this realm, and in the spiritual realm, and all of these miraculous connections take place within your very brain.

The place that I am referring to rests at the center of your brain, in between the two hemispheres. It's located at the top of your spinal cord and is directly behind your pituitary gland. The name of this special, sacred place is the pineal gland.

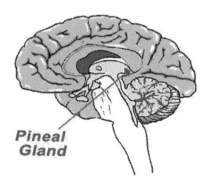

Pineal Gland

(source: Wikipedia)

The Third Eye and Its Threats

When I first discovered the pineal (pronounced: pine kneel) gland and began to understand all of its complex and magical workings, I felt as if I had struck gold. And interestingly enough that is exactly what a properly functioning, unclogged pineal gland secretes—a form of liquid gold. René Descartes, the seventeenth-century French philosopher mathematician, concluded after his own extensive investigations that the pineal gland was the seat of the soul. He believed that it was the point of connection between the intellect and the body.

His ideas, no matter how archaic they may sound to us today, still hold true. The amazing capacity of the pineal gland to form beautiful connections has only proven even more fascinating through the inquiries of modern research.

The pineal gland is quite small, only about the size of a pea, and is shaped like a tiny pinecone, which reveals the origins of its name. The pineal gland is often referred to as the "third eye" and is considered the gateway to spirituality and higher consciousness. Every human and most animals except for some mammals and invertebrates have a pineal gland. The pineal gland is the primary gland that forms in the fetus as it is developing in utero, and does so at the rapid speed of approximately three weeks.

Despite the power and magic of the pineal gland, by the age of seventeen, on average 40% of Americans have a calcified pineal. This means that a large percentage of the population in the United States will have difficulty gaining valuable insight and creativity from their higher self, source, and the universe before entering adulthood. The calcification of the pineal gland can often be attributed to: fluoride found in water and toothpaste; and consumption (on a regular basis) of carbonated sodas, dairy, meat, and processed foods.

When the pineal gland becomes calcified and hardened, it will actually show up on x-rays. Fluoride, a common substance, is the primary toxin that can cause this devastating result. It's widely known that fluoride is an extremely neurotoxic chemical and is the active ingredient found in rat poison and in Prozac. Fluoride interrupts the basic function of nerve cells in the brain, resulting in docile, submissive behavior and a lowering of natural IQ levels. Furthermore, calcification of the pineal gland blocks people from tapping into their intuition and inner knowing, and can lead to having a defective sense of direction.

Needless to say, fluoride is harmful to your mind and body. The only way to eliminate fluoride from your tap water is through the process of reverse osmosis, which also strips away vital minerals from the water. You should only boil water that *doesn't* contain fluoride, since the boiling process actually concentrates the fluoride. Avoiding fluoride is especially important for children, since it has been proven to alter the appearance of children's teeth during development. It's perfectly acceptable to decline a fluoride rinse after having your teeth cleaned at the dentist, as I choose to do. I only use natural toothpaste that is void of fluoride, sugar, and other synthetic chemicals.

While researching the pineal gland, I came across a wealth of information regarding fluoride and its damaging effects on the pineal gland, which could be one reason for the water fluorination conspiracy websites. I personally am not fond of wasting time or energy so I choose to not spend time on conspiracy theories; however, I always advocate for doing your own research and arriving at your own conclusions. Take into consideration your needs, and remember the important fact that the pineal gland only functions well when its not clogged.

How can you know if your pineal gland is clogged? I suggest that you perform the following self-assessment:

- Are you often tired throughout the day?
- Do you have trouble sleeping at night?
- Are you often forgetful?
- Do you feel foggy headed during the day?
- Do you have trouble thinking creatively?
- Do you have difficulty tapping into your intuition or gut feelings?
- Do you have difficulty quieting your mind and focusing your thoughts?
- Do you look older than your actual age?
- Do you have difficulty remembering your dreams?
- Do you have a low sex drive?

If you answered "yes" to at least seven of those questions, the chances are high that you do in fact have a clogged pineal gland.

The good news is that pineal glands can be unclogged and returned to proper functioning order, which I will outline later in the chapter. First though, you must understand the workings of the pineal gland in order to best tackle the challenges of healing it.

Inside the Pineal Gland

Your pineal is considered the master gland of the endocrine system. A gland is a group of cells that produces and secretes, or gives off, chemicals. A gland selects and removes materials from the blood, processes them, and secretes the finished chemical product for use somewhere in the body. The pineal gland secretes melatonin, which is a precursor to serotonin. This function helps to regulate the balancing act of the wake-sleep cycle. The production of melatonin by the pineal gland is stimulated by darkness. That's why it's imperative to get adequate sleep. I would recommend doing so in a dark room, and not allowing any light to enter for the highest efficiency.

Melatonin is a powerful antioxidant that's not inhibited by the blood brain barrier. It has the capacity to absorb free radicals. In animal studies, melatonin has been proven to prevent damage done to DNA by certain carcinogens, in some cases stopping cancer from developing. Furthermore, melatonin has been demonstrated to prolong the average life of lab mice by 20%. You may think that it would be a quick fix to run out and purchase over the counter melatonin at your local drug store, but you should reconsider. The melatonin that's sold as a dietary supplement is actually extracted from the pineal glands of animals, mostly cows. Animals that are fed diets from genetically modified foods such as corn are often malnourished. They have a high level of toxic buildup in their pineal gland. Therefore I recommend steering clear of any melatonin dietary supplements and simply working toward decalcifying and nourishing your pineal gland through your own natural methods.

The pineal gland functions best when your body is receiving a proper balance of light and dark. This balance brings to mind the *yin* and *yang*, which symbolize masculine and feminine energy. Both are in need of one another to be in harmony. After all, your pineal gland is located in the center of your brain, and the most recent studies suggest it contains up to three hundred tiny micro-crystals. These micro-crystals vary in terms of size, number and color depending upon your mission in life, and also upon the frequency at which you vibrate.

This discovery is not a surprise, since recently it has also been discovered that at the center of the Earth is a giant crystal, over 1.5 miles in diameter, rather than the iron ore that was previously believed to occupy that space. The Earth's core crystal is *anisotropic*, which means it has a directional quality to it. In fact, that's why it has been documented that energy moves faster north to south and slower east to west.

The crystals in our pineal gland connect us to the Earth and also to everyone we meet. This connection allows us to communicate telepathically with living beings and with those who have already graduated, or passed on from this realm. This connection to others via the pineal gland and the crystals within is why when you think of someone, they too think of you. Think back to how many times you thought of someone and right then the phone rang and that very person you were thinking of was on the other end of the line and you both laughed and chalked it up to coincidence.

Let's continue. The pineal gland is not susceptible to the blood brain barrier, and thus it flourishes when fed a rich source of blood, oxygen and nutrients. These important ingredients are most notably found in super foods and spring water. As the pineal gland secretes melatonin, it activates the pituitary gland to release melanocyte-stimulating hormone, more commonly referred to as MSH. It's within the MSH that melanin is produced.

Melanin is the key to having and maintaining supernatural abilities. Melanin actually enhances intelligence and emotional and spiritual sensitivity. With proper melanin levels, you will have the ability to reach higher levels of performance and maintain high energy levels. Melanin allows one to transform solar energy, electro-magnetic energy, electricity, microwaves, music/sound waves, radar, waves, radio TV waves, thermal waves X-rays, cosmic rays, and UV light into more useful energy such as kinetic energy.

Melanin also gives one the ability to relieve the brain from its responsibility of bodily coordination. It can also supervise physiological functions without the need to report to the brain. This frees up the brain's resources to concentrate on more important matters such as intellectual, emotional and spiritual pursuits.

Melanin can provide one with the ability to delay the aging process, and can help to protect us from the development of skin cancer. This is because melanin found in the skin protects against harmful ultra-violet rays of the sun by absorbing the UV rays and converting it into harmless heat.

Lastly, but perhaps most importantly, melanin has the miraculous ability to duplicate itself, regardless of nutrients.

Nourishing and Decalcifying the Pineal Gland

You can increase your levels of melanin by eating certain foods that stimulate your body to produce the chemical. Such foods are those that are high in copper, vitamin D, and vitamin E. Chaga mushrooms are an excellent source to stimulate the production of melanin as well as cacao (pronounced "kuh kow"), not to be confused with cocoa since cacao is chocolate in its raw natural form. Cacao is a super antioxidant and works miracles on the body and pineal gland (more on this in the next chapter).

Dark grapes, black olives, noni fruit and organic raw foods are also excellent for the workings of the pineal gland and the production of melanin. Avoiding factory-farmed meat, processed food, genetically modified foods, refined sugar, sodas, fish (especially those with a high mercury content such as tuna), white flour, carbonated beverages, and non-organic dairy is essential for maintaining a healthy pineal.

Before we can stimulate and nourish your pineal we must first make sure that its decalcified. You can reverse calcification of the pineal gland, but it takes intention and diligence, and requires considerable time and a healthy diet. Before you undertake this task, you must determine that you truly want to live longer, look younger, be smarter, be happier, have better focus, be more creative, and have a better connection to your higher self, to others, to the planet and to the spiritual realm. Once you have made the commitment to bring about those positive results, you will be more ready to take on the challenge of decalcification.

There are certain supplements and herbal remedies that you can utilize to aid the process. Liquid Zeolite, when taken regularly, will help escort heavy metals and toxins out of the pineal, as will super foods such as chlorella, spirulina, and seaweed that has been sun-dried and therefore has concentrated vitamin D, such as dulse, nori and kombu. Most of these varieties can be found in the grocery store and are excellent to include in protein or power shakes. Oils rich in vitamin K2 are essential for decalcifying the pineal gland. The best choice is fermented skate fish (sometimes labeled as rat fish) oil found in capsules. Skate fish are bottom feeders and produce nutrient rich oil from their liver. This oil is high in EFA, or essential fatty acids, and high in vitamins C, D, E and K2. These are all able to effectively remove toxins and heavy metals from the body, while continuing to nourish the functions of the pineal gland. You will want to take these capsules at night before going to bed because you don't want to burp skate liver oil throughout the day, trust me on this!

The pineal gland also is involved in the vital actions of the memory. If the gland becomes overly exhausted, you will notice patterns of forgetfulness in your day-to-day life. As you begin to give energy and nutrients back to the pineal gland through the process of decalcification, you'll notice an improvement in your ability to recall both short- and long-term memories.

As I mentioned above, sleeping in a dark room is essential for restoring and resting the pineal gland. It's also imperative to expose your body to an adequate amount of direct sunlight during the day in order to absorb a satisfactory amount of vitamin D. It's ideal if you can absorb the light through your naked eyes in an outdoor setting. Take it slow and start out in the morning or evening when the sun is less intense. Looking into the sun for fifteen seconds at the outset is optimal, and then gradually build up to a minute of sun intake during each exercise. To fully engage the pineal gland, sunlight should be taken in and digested through the eyes, skin, hair, nose hairs, and ears for a minimum of thirty minutes a day.

Activating and Connecting the Pineal Gland

Once nourished, restored and functioning properly, the next step is to activate the powerhouse potential of the pineal gland. You can activate your pineal gland through prayer, meditation, breathing exercises, super foods, uninterrupted sleep, fasting, dancing, singing, passionate love making, creative visualization or anything else that can help you get in touch with your inner self.

Connecting your mind and body with your spiritual or kundalini energy, is a valuable function of the pineal gland. When you meditate with your back straight and your head held upright, you're allowing for a direct connection to be formed between the different energy centers, or chakras, contained within your body. This makes it possible for the golden fluid secreted by the pineal gland to travel via the spinal cord, reaching all the chakras and extending to the base of the spine. There, the golden fluid will begin pooling with the kundalini energy, flowing back up with the powerful energy through the 33 energy points of the spine to the pineal gland, all while moving in a snake-like fashion.

The energy moving looks something like this:

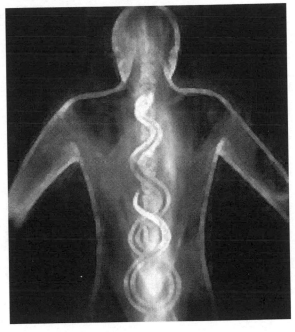

This process of sitting in meditation while thinking of loving sexual thoughts, or thinking of something that inspires you, or that makes you feel connected to nature activates the kundalini energy. This process only works when you have a clear intention of activating your pineal gland. When the kundalini energy is activated it flows through the spinal cord to the pineal gland, activating the third eye in a profound way that you will want to duplicate over and over. You might feel a bit lightheaded while attempting to open your third eye this way, or you might even feel a slight throbbing in the region of your third eye, which rests in between your two physical eyes above your eyebrows. It may be helpful to remember that the third eye is a muscle that can be developed with practice. The more you exercise the muscle of your third eye, or inner vision, the better you will be at receiving information regarding any and all subjects.

When the third eye, or pineal gland, is truly activated in this way, it may seem as though you've been granted the keys to the kingdom. You will now have any and all information, wisdom and insight available to you via your higher self. Once you're able to tap into your intuitive nature, you'll find that you sleep better, feel better, can act with more love and confidence, and have an improved sex drive.

You'll feel primed to embark once again, fresh and ready along your own path to true success. You may experience connections to other human beings that you had only dreamed of, both in physical relationships and in spiritual understandings of others, both living and deceased. You will notice that you're better able to remember your dreams, whether they are those experienced in sleep or those that come back to your from your past, encouraging you to restart plans that you have let go of and seize the important moments of your life.

You'll experience a higher level of creativity, and be able to focus your thoughts on the present moment. The hidden powers of the pineal gland are vital and magical, but in fact they are no secret. Your untapped potential is waiting to be discovered, all within the beautiful and ever- expanding landscape of your mind, body and spirit.

✸ SELF-ASSESSMENT

♦ Open your refrigerator. Look at the foods you have stored there, and in your pantry or cupboards too. How many of these foods and beverages contain processed ingredients? Sugar? White flour? Corn syrup? Preservatives? These foods are clogging your pineal gland, not to mention causing other harmful effects. Get rid of them. Eat fresh organic wholesome foods, avoid fluoridated water, and get out into the sunshine. You'll feel the difference!

♦ A terrific way to start eating healthier is to first become aware of the quality (or lack of) foods you are currently consuming. You can do this by starting a food journal.

Write down in your journal all the food, snacks and drinks you consume throughout the day. Study your journal weekly and determine if you are making the best possible food choices for yourself and your body. This awareness will help you see what changes you need to make to your diet in order to feel healthier and feel more alive and focused.

Chapter 12:
Improving Your Health
Benefits More Than Your
Body

"If you don't take care of your body,
where are you going to live?"
~ Anonymous

Don't worry I'm not going to tell you to stop all your unhealthy habits, eat bland food and work out like a fiend. Nope, I won't do that to you, I promise. What I will do though is give you a quick run down on how your body works, and what you can do to improve your health and increase your energy. Then I'll leave the rest to you. Fair enough?

Here's the truth. When your mind—body—spirit is healthy and working together harmoniously you'll experience the most abundant, joyful and prosperous life you can ever imagine. In this chapter, I assist you in discovering how your intentions, food choices, stress levels; exercise, breath and flexibility can heal and influence your mind body spirit. I share the steps of how you can change your physical body (matter) at a cellular level, and also how to increase your ability to focus and think clearly. Furthermore, I'll share how to increase your energy sustainably and quickly, without the use of caffeine or sugar. My hope is this chapter enlightens and inspires you to take simple steps that can change your body and life from the inside out.

Since this book has to do with having success in life, I'll only share aspects of the body and its functions that contribute directly to your success and wellbeing. I strive for simplicity in my life and in my work, so what could potentially be a really complicated topic I have done my best to simplify... let's get started.

Your cells are the very building blocks of life, they reproduce, retain energy, have consciousness, intelligence and memory. Your body is host to trillions of cells, each of which have purpose, consciousness and the ability to remember. Furthermore, with recent advancements in science and technology it has been discovered that all of your cells have the ability to communicate with one another and respond to your thoughts. Cells also have a set of "little organs," called organelles that are adapted and/or specialized for carrying out one or more vital functions. (Amer. Naturalist. 23, 1889, Möbius)

Mitochondria is the cell's powerhouse, generating energy for the cell in the form of adenosine triphosphate (ATP) by using oxygen to release energy stored in cellular nutrients (typically pertaining to glucose). ATP is what gives you energy to function and is the main energy source for the majority of cellular functions. ATP supplies most of the body's energy as well as your blood and oxygen flow, and your body uses oxygen to produce energy, thus completing the energy flow cycle. Interrupting the body's flow of energy happens two ways: first, when the body doesn't get exercise, and second, when fatty foods are consumed. Both of which create build up in arteries and that inhibits blood and oxygen flow to vital organs, the pineal gland and throughout the body.

Research has shown lack of exercise is more detrimental to a body's health than smoking. Sufficient exercise can come from walking thirty minutes a day five times a week, doing yoga, taking the stairs instead of the elevator, parking far away from your building, even deep breathing while stretching is excellent for your body. I'm sure you've heard a body in motion stays in motion and a body at rest stays at rest. This is a basic saying that applies to most everything. It is also why the first two weeks of starting an exercise program is difficult because your body isn't used to being in motion. However, after your body is use to being in motion, exercise will start to feel like a treat rather than a chore. Let's continue.

Veins carry blood to the heart to be filtered and oxygenated by your lungs. Filtered and oxygenated rich blood gets carried from the heart throughout the body by arteries. Exercising and a diet high in fiber and essential nutrients will help keep your veins working optimally and your arties clog free, both of which are essential to feeling and looking good.

Stress and Its Effect on Your Body

When your body is stressed your breathing slows (or becomes shallow) which restricts the blood, oxygen and nutrient flow to your vital organs and to your brain. Exercise and deep breathing play a crucial role in your body's ability to maintain high energy levels. How many times have you been doing something while holding your breath? A friend of mine, Frederic Leyd, inventor of The Two-Minute Back Solution (Google him, he's terrific), helps people heal themselves and their bodies quickly. He and I were talking recently and he said something that really struck me: "Breath is the range of motion in the mind. The looser you are in your mind the looser your body will be."

He and I both agree that holding your breath creates tension in the body that can lead to injury and at the very least stops your creative juices from flowing. Deep breathing several times a day allows for your blood to become more oxygenated and nutrient rich. Furthermore, an abundant blood flow not only provides your body nutrients, it also takes away waste products. The key is in doing the things that help keep your arteries dilated and your blood pumping. What's good for your heart and arteries, in essence, is good for your energy levels, too. Exercise, sex, deep breathing, eating healthy, yoga and meditating increase blood flow as well.

Blood flow is the single most important thing for your brain to function optimally. Blood delivers glucose to your brain, which is used as energy. Your brain uses 20% of the blood flow from every heartbeat. Improving blood flow to your brain will improve you brainpower. Of course things such as smoking, eating junk food and drinking caffeinated beverages constrict arteries, which after time actually shrink the size of your brain. Remember, what's healthy for your heart is healthy for your brain.

Your pH Level

Your body is a delicate system of checks and balances. One way to quickly and easily determine your body's overall health is to measure its pH level. Your body's pH level is an indicator of just how well your body is functioning. Strips that test your urine or saliva can be purchased at any health food store or online. The strips measure your body's alkalinity and acid balance. Keeping your body more alkaline and less acidic will make you feel better, become more agile and perform better. Conversely, when pH levels in the body are out of balance, disease or dis-ease (the syllable spacing is intentional to illustrate what disease really is, and that is dis-ease or dis-comfort in the body) within the body can occur and can result in a series of health issues. However, when the body's pH is restored to proper balance, the body's health can be more effectively restored.

As a general rule, almost all vegetables, fruits, mineral water, and sea salt have an alkalinizing effect on the body. Conversely, almost all animal proteins, whole grains, beans, dairy, alcohol, and sugars have an acidic effect on the body. Optimally, your diet would consist of foods that are 80% alkaline and 20% acid in terms of how they are processed within your body. By doing so you can achieve a balanced pH (6.5 to 8.0). Interestingly enough, foods that taste acidic such as citrus fruits have an alkalinizing effect on the body. Putting lemon drops in your water is a quick way to alkalize water and is wonderful for your body.

A quick Internet search will yield multiple sites with detailed lists of alkaline and acidic foods.

Stay Balanced

An essential truth to good health is to avoid at all costs those things that cause the body to become imbalanced. Here are some things to avoid.

♦ Ingesting toxic substances such as certain foods, alcohol, cigarettes and drugs.

♦ Breathing in air pollution.

♦ Negative environment such as a stressful work place or home.

♦ Negative thoughts or feelings such as excess worry or fear.

Clearly, the mind and body are directly linked, and when you overload your system with toxic thoughts and feelings your body produces more acid and becomes unbalanced, and is then susceptible to illness or disease. I learned firsthand, how being imbalanced effects the body the year I turned 30.

When your body is out of balance, it shows first on your largest organ, your skin. When I was thirty years old, I developed acne! It was awful and embarrassing, and since I am an overachiever I developed acne in a big way. Not the little tiny pimples that people get around their nose or on their forehead; no, I had large cystic acne on my cheeks. I had never experienced acne as a teenager, so I had no idea how to deal with it or what to do to alleviate the condition. Instinctually, I knew that taking medication wasn't the right path for solving my problem. I wanted to heal my body naturally, but first I had to figure out the cause of my acne.

At the time I was living in southern California near Beverly Hills, and I knew that if I asked around I would find someone who could help me. Eventually, I was guided to a spa on Sunset Boulevard. Little did I know then that this simple visit to a spa would result in a dramatic change that would impact me for the rest of my life.

At the spa, I met a man named Ole Henricksen. Ole is a gregarious Danish man with an infectious laugh and a warm smile. Ole shared with me a very personal story that resonated deeply within me and was a catalyst for my growth. When he was younger and traveled throughout the world, living the high life and engaging in a lifestyle of partying and excess, he developed acne. He, too, was led to seek a holistic clinic that treated his acne by various natural botanicals, which inspired him to move to London and study skin care. After experimenting with various raw, organic materials in his kitchen and mastering his craft, he moved to Beverly Hills with the intention to help people heal their skin naturally. Ole often wowed me with stories of his celebrity clients, but more importantly, he shared with me a valued and well-kept secret about skin care.

Now, have you ever heard something that resonated with you so deeply that you knew in that very moment your life would be forever changed? If you said "yes," you'll relate to the feeling I had when he revealed the secret to great skin. He said, "Great skin comes from the inside out." He then continued by revealing that acne is a warning sign indicating that something is imbalanced within the body and needs correcting or else something much worse can develop in time. For me, this was major news. I was thirty years old and up until that time I didn't give much thought to what I applied topically to my skin, and even less thought to the quality (or lack thereof) of the foods I ingested.

This awakening to the body/food connection started me on the path to eating healthy. Ole told me it would take at least a year for my body to correct the imbalance, and he was right; however, within a few short months of improving my diet I started losing excess weight, had more energy, and looked really fit even though I didn't work out very much. Ever since then, eating healthy has always been a priority for me; especially during times of stress since I am prone to eating sugar, which completely throws my mind and body into a spin. Emotionally I become erratic when I eat a few cookies, not to mention I can feel my insulin spiking as my heart races and I stress out my adrenals. All in all it's not a healthy feeling! For more information on the damaging effects sugar has on your body, I highly recommend the book *Sugar Blues* by William Dufty.

You are probably aware when certain foods affect your body in a not so pleasing way. Hopefully you are listening to your body and becoming aware of what it's trying to tell you. Almost everyone will benefit from eating a healthy, mostly alkaline diet and the benefits (sustained energy, less joint inflammation, better blood circulation etc.) can be felt almost immediately.

You might wonder, "How do I know which foods are best for me?" The best way to know for sure is go by how you feel thirty minutes to an hour after a meal. If you feel energized, then whatever you ate was a great choice. However, if you feel tired, bloated, or are still hungry then your body didn't get enough nutrients and it's letting you know by the unpleasant feelings. Your body needs a variety of foods and vegetables to function optimally, the easiest way to figure out what it needs is go to the grocery store, stand in the produce section, and look at all the fruits and vegetables. Your eyes will communicate with your stomach and your body will tell you what it needs based on what foods you feel drawn to.

Also, foods that are colorful and that have the same colors that are found in rainbows (red, orange, yellow, blue, green, indigo and violet) are high in antioxidants.

Another way to easily determine the foods that are right for your body is to bring a friend along to the grocery store and muscle test for the right foods. Muscle testing is a sure proof way of figuring out what's right for your body, and it's easy to do. Here's how: hold a fruit or vegetable in your hand and bring it to the center of your chest, close to your heart. Now, hold your other arm straight out and shoulder high and see if your friend can easily push it down. If your friend is able to push your arm down easily then that food is not the right choice for you. However, if your friend has difficulty lowering your arm than your food choice resonates with your body.

By the way, muscle testing can help you figure out a lot of things not just what foods are right for you. Give it a shot and let me know how it worked for you.

Cellular Change—With the Power of Thought

Whether you're awake or asleep, your cells are in constant motion performing their "jobs" automatically and are always on alert to feedback coming from you *via* your thoughts, words and intentions. Yes, your cells respond to you and will do what you want them to do given the right environment, which is created by a healthy body. Just as the universe responds to your thoughts so do your cells, and that's why it's *uber*-important for you to be aware of your thoughts, inner dialogue, and spoken words when it comes to you. All words carry a "charge" or vibration. This vibration is felt throughout your body as you speak and as you listen to others speak. Your body's internal organs, cells, skin, heart, brain, muscles, tissue, hair, and bones are listening to your every word. Words are powerful and can have a powerful effect on your body.

That being said, if there is something about your body you would like to change, you can do this by your clear intentions, focused thoughts and spoken words.

I personally know this works because when I was in my early twenties I had a pencil-thin upper lip that I wasn't particularly fond of. Intuitively I knew I could increase the size of my upper lip by just using my thoughts. And every day for two weeks I asked my upper lip to grow thicker by focusing my thoughts and attention and gratitude on having a thicker upper lip. Next, I spent time every day (about five minutes) visualizing myself with a thicker upper lip. Within two weeks I felt movement in my lip, which felt odd at first, sort of like growth happening from the inside out. The process was quick; it only took a couple of minutes and soon after I had a thicker upper lip. I believe it's permanent too, since its been over twenty years and my lip is still thicker.

From that experience I got really excited because I realized I could change my physical body by just using the power of my thoughts and mind. Since that time I have "instructed" my body to do many things, such as: wake me up at a specific time without the need for setting an alarm, sleep peacefully and soundly, thicken the muscles in my legs, release love handles, improve my eyesight, thicken the hair on my head and face, and even lower my body temperature. Now, I don't know the exact science behind how these changes happened; however, I do know, you too can change your physical body as long as the conditions are ripe. Which means the pH in your body is balanced and healthy, and your thoughts are focused and concentrated on what you desire.... All you have to do is tell your body what to do, your cells are listening and will respond to your request.

Transform Yourself With Raw Foods

You have probably had the experience of your body feeling sluggish and tired after eating certain foods. For most this happens in the afternoon, especially after eating a big lunch. Food has the ability to alter your moods, change how you feel, give you energy, and even heal your body.

Nutritious foods that aren't cooked to death can have an amazing impact on your level of energy and your ability to feel unstoppable. Raw foods are defined as food that is in its natural state and not cooked at a temperature above 118 degrees

Fahrenheit. That's important because at approximately 118 degrees Fahrenheit the molecular structure of food changes and so does your body's ability to process it.

The moment food passes over your lips and you begin to chew, your saliva sends messages to your stomach alerting your stomach which acids to prepare to aid in digestion. The more you chew your food the more alkaline it becomes in your mouth, so chew each bite at least sixteen times and eat slowly. This will help you digest.

Now, when you eat a meal that is 100% cooked something very interesting happens in your body. This was tested and documented at the Institute of Clinical Chemistry in Lausanne, Switzerland, under the direction of Dr. Paul Kouchakoff. Dr. Kouchakoff's discovery concerned leukocytes (the white blood cells). It was found that after a person eats cooked food, his or her blood responds immediately by increasing the number of white blood cells. No one knew why the number of white cells would rise. It appeared to be a stress response, as if the body were reacting to something harmful, such as exposure to toxic chemicals, an infection, or some sort of trauma. While studying the influence of food on human blood, they made a remarkable discovery. They found that eating raw food, or food heated at low temperatures, did not cause any reaction in the blood. In addition, if a food had been heated beyond a certain temperature (unique to each food), or if the food was processed (refined, chemicals added, etc.), this always caused a rise in the number of white blood cells. They tested many different kinds of foods and again found that if the foods were not overheated or refined, they caused no such reaction. The body merely saw them as "friendly foods." However, if these same foods were heated above 118 degrees Fahrenheit, these same foods caused a negative reaction in the blood, a reaction similar to when the body is invaded by a dangerous pathogen or experiences some sort of trauma.

The job of white blood cells is to fight disease, kill bacteria, combat allergic reactions, and destroy old or damaged cells. White blood cells have feet, ears and eyes; they can communicate messages to other cells; they have memory; and they are even capable of sharing what they remember with other cells. In other words they are smart and conscious. Furthermore, Dr. Kouchakoff discovered, meals that were made up of foods that were at least 51% raw did not cause a rise in white blood cells and the cells did not go into stress related attack mode.

That's a strong case for eating foods in their natural raw state. Here are a few things you can do to start improving your body's health and wellbeing. First, ease into eating raw foods. If you go 100% raw overnight you might be making a big mistake, because you could actually do more harm than good by overly taxing your liver with "old sludge" and toxins that have been in your system for years. Raw foods act like a roto-rooter to your system, cleaning out your body and your cells quickly; but you could experience detoxification effects such as diarrhea and nausea, neither of which are fun. I suggest adding to your dinner plate half raw food (maybe a bit more than half to get your plate to 51% raw) and healthy cooked foods on the other side. Eat this way for two months or so and see how you feel. More than likely you'll start to feel great, then over time slowly add more raw foods and fewer cooked foods to your diet.

Raw Super Foods

A few delicious and nutritious raw foods that are high in protein are: spinach, kale, avocado, sprouts, broccoli, Brazilian nuts, hemp seeds, chia seeds, savi seeds, figs, goji-berries and spirulina. Many of these amazing foods are also considered super foods, and I'll get to those shortly; for now just know, any and all of the above are the most optimal choices for protein in your diet as each one has alkalinizing effects on your body and all are easily converted into amino acids, which are the essential building blocks of muscle. All vegetables have protein and salads help lodge protein into the body's tissues. If you think about it, the biggest, strongest land animals such as elephants, gorillas, hippos, moose and bulls are all vegetarians and don't eat meat.

Raw Food Recipes

Some people find it difficult to start eating foods raw. For some it might be a psychological hurdle and for others a taste issue. For those who have a taste issue, it's due to your taste buds becoming addicted to foods that are either fried, fatty, sweet, salty or loaded with sauces. Your taste buds have forgotten how food tastes in its natural form.

Let's remind the body what good nutrition tastes like, shall we? A very simple and easy way to get the body to consume raw foods is by juicing them. There are many options on the market for juicers, the most optimal are juicers made by Champion and are actually presses.

Presses are ideal because they don't heat up the food (change its chemical structure) during the juicing process. (Just email me at jaden@jadensterling.com if you have specific questions about juicers. I'm happy to answer your questions.) Presses are optimal for getting the most nutrients from your fruits and vegetables. For example, carrots have an essential enzyme that's only released when pressed with apples.

Starting your day drinking fresh carrot juice could very well change your life! Carrot juice is loaded with beta-carotene, which produces vitamin A and E in the body which improves eyesight and helps strengthen bones, prevents cancer, and helps you look younger. When juicing or pressing carrots keep the skin on, as it's loaded with vitamins and minerals.

A simple, delicious and healthy breakfast that takes less than five minutes to make is:

Organic Instant Harmony Juice (Serves 2):

Juice/press (organic when possible):

8 carrots

2 beets

2 apples, small to medium (seeds are ok)

2 leaves of kale (stalk included)

1 lemon wedge

1" ginger

Juice the fruits and vegetables in the same order as I have listed above. This juice tastes great and has amazing cellular restorative effects. You'll know this to be true the moment you taste this drink and all your cells do a happy dance, you'll see. Now, to really super charge this drink add a teaspoon of chlorella to the juice, stir and drink.

For lunch or dinner another wonderful raw food recipe "Tacos." Blend in a mixer using the S blade (that's the blade shaped like an S)—to make the sauce:

3 tbsp walnuts

2 tsp fresh lemon juice

1 tbsp olive oil (first cold pressed extra virgin)

1 tbsp tahini

¼ cup coconut water (best from a coconut; however, packaged coconut water will work fine too).

Mix all ingredients until smooth.

Then put butter lettuce on a plate and add zucchini strips, carrot slices, broccoli sprouts, strips of basil, and sliced grape tomatoes on top of the butter lettuce, but leave room so you can fold the lettuce and make little "tacos." Lastly, add pine nuts and sauce on top and enjoy!

For dessert, if your family likes chocolate this recipe could possibly end up becoming your family's favorite healthy dessert. I call this "The Greatest Chocolate Mousse On The Planet," it's delicious and simple to make.

In your food processor using the S blade combine:

½ avocado

7 tbsp of cacao (Not cocoa—cacao is chocolate in its raw and natural form.)

4 tbsp honey

1 ½ tsp powdered organic vanilla

3 pinches of sea salt (never table salt)

Blend on high until it's light and smooth. This dessert can be eaten right away or put in the refrigerator and saved for later.

There are many Internet sites that have great raw food recipes. Some of my favorites are:

♦ http://adeleengel.healthcoach.integrativenutrition.com

♦ http://rawfoodrecipes.com

♦ http://www.rawmazing.com/rawmazing-recipes/

Sprouts are another amazing alive food that your body will love and are easy to grow right in your own kitchen or buy from any grocery store. When something has the ability to sprout that means it's alive as opposed to foods that are cooked or are dead to begin with.

In our house we sprout broccoli seeds, sunflower seeds, chickpeas, and lentils regularly. They are healthy, delicious and easy to grow.

To start all you need are raw, organic seeds, beans or peas. The lentils and beans can be placed in a bowl covered with spring water and put in the refrigerator. The seeds, however, need to be placed in a mason jar covered with a screen or cheesecloth and left in a cool dark cupboard to grow. Each day rinse the seeds, beans or lentils and add more spring water. After a day or so you'll start to see your food growing and sprouting; it's really quite something!

Experiment on your own and have fun with this.

Soon you'll start to look and feel great and any excess weight will drop off quickly.

Before I switch gears and talk about super foods, I want to share with you a terrific resource when it comes to the healing effects that raw foods and juicing have on the body, and her name is Charlotte Gerson. When you have time, I recommend watching some interviews of her on YouTube; she is in her nineties and is quite fascinating and knowledgeable.

Super Foods for Super Success

As you raise your awareness and consciousness to the effects that certain foods have on your body, you'll naturally gravitate toward solutions that continue to give you amazing results. The results you can expect to achieve by making better food choices are less inflammation in your joints, better mental clarity and focus, more energy, better moods, and an overall feeling of wellbeing and peace within your body, mind and soul. As your health and vitality improves you'll naturally seek out solutions to continue increasing your health and raising your energy.

Those who have been on a mostly raw food meal plan for at least six months are ready to experience the power of "super foods." Super foods take your physical and mental health to a level you never knew was possible. Super foods nourish your body and increase your life force or chi energy beyond anything else. A leader and pioneer in this field is David Wolfe. He has lots of videos on YouTube to help educate people to the benefits of super foods. The guy's energy is amazing and never once have I ever seen him yawn!

Super foods have been around for centuries, are found all over the world, and have medicinal benefits for your body. I must share a warning with you similar to the one I regarding raw foods: don't do what my wife and I did and jump into raw/super foods with both feet! Start slowly. We are both type A's and go all out whenever we do anything and our foray into super foods was no different. The first 10 days I was exclusively on super foods and raw foods I lost eight pounds and made no less than ten trips to the bathroom each day. Thankfully I work from home and wasn't travelling at the time, so I had easy access to the restroom, but boy it was intense. Okay, you've been forewarned!

Amazing things began happening for me when I started eating super foods. One thing happened that was an unintended (yet welcomed) consequence... I healed my depression. You see, my mother had graduated (passed on) into the spiritual realm unexpectedly. I wasn't emotionally prepared for her passing - it was the fifth of my close family members and loved ones who had "graduated" within four years. I felt lost and couldn't shake the tight hold depression had on me.

I couldn't even recognize myself: I had lost my sense of humor, I was rapidly gaining weight, I was unmotivated, and at one point I was even afraid to leave the house for fear I would burst into tears unexpectedly. I experienced what I referred to as, the *cumulative sorrow effect*, since I never dealt with my twin brother's passing from cancer two years prior.

A month after my mother's passing, my wife asked me to go to an event and hear Deepak Chopra speak. Normally I would jump at the chance; however, I was really suffering from depression during that time and I wasn't really interested in going, but I went. During that event I also heard David Wolfe speak, and he shared how super foods can really help change your life. I figured my life needed changing and fast, so on our way home we stopped at a health food store and picked up what he recommended: goji-berries, cacao beans and cacao nibs, chlorella, spirulina, red maca, bee pollen honey, blue-green algae, almond butter, a good probiotic, coconut oil, organic walnuts, almonds, sunflower seeds, pumpkin seeds, and his book, *Superfoods*.

Within a few days of eating raw foods and taking super foods, my body felt lighter and became lighter as the excess weight I was carrying dropped off in a matter of days. Little did I know I had found just the thing that would help me get out of my funk, lose weight, revitalize my body and nourish my brain beyond anything I had ever experienced before. I am passionate about sharing with people how impactful food is when it comes to experiencing success. We've all heard the saying, "what good is money if you don't have your health?" However, how many people are spending the time necessary to nourish their body, mind and spirit properly? Just giving you food for thought.

After months of experimenting with many different super foods and super herbs my family and I have discovered our favorites. The super foods that we enjoy the most are: blue-green algae, Chaga and Reishi mushrooms, maca, tocotrienols, schizandra, lucuma, honey, marine phytoplankton, cacao, spirulina, chlorella, goji-berries, noni, hemp seeds, cacao butter, coconut oil, and Udo's oil 3-6-9 Blend. Brief benefits of the above are as follows, per David Wolfe's book titled, *Superfoods*: "Blue-green algae (Aphanizomenon flos-aquae AFA) are made primarily of soft proteins and polysaccharides that are easily digested by our intestinal bacteria that in turn then feed our blood and cells. This 'softness' makes AFA one of the most digestible and utilizable protein foods in all of nature."

AFA is loaded with chlorophyll, which helps build our blood and feed our brains. AFA is also an amazing source of B vitamins which help fight stress by helping to efficiently convert polysaccharides and other carbohydrates into glucose which is what gives the body stamina, energy and endurance. A teaspoon of blue-green algae mixed with cold water or added to any shake tastes delicious and will immediately boost your energy levels. Other greens include two of my favorites, spirulina and chlorella. Spirulina is an algae super food that contains the highest concentration of protein found in any food. It is a complete protein source containing all eight essential amino acids. It is also rich in beta-carotene, B vitamins and vitamin K, which is essential for a healthy pineal gland. Protein is essential for building muscle, strength and endurance and this plant-based source is one of the best as it has all the amino acids to build stronger muscles without the fat content or harmful toxic chemicals often given to protein sources. Furthermore, Dr. Gabriel Cousens sites research from the Max Planck Institute regarding protein and says, "50% of the protein in food is lost after it is cooked." That being said, protein content of any food source that is cooked is half of what the label indicates. Spirulina is a pure raw source of protein that has never been cooked nor does it need to be.

Maca is a root super food grown in high altitudes in the Peruvian Andes for more than 2,600 years. Maca is a powerful strength and stamina enhancer and also is libido enhancing. Maca not only increases energy, endurance, and oxygen in the blood but it also supports the endocrine system, adrenals and thyroid, and improves one's overall mood. Adding maca to any shake is delicious and fortifying.

Next are our favorite sweeteners that are also nutrient dense and have health enhancing benefits. Lucuma is from the "egg fruit" of Peru and in powdered form makes a tasty and creamy addition to any shake. Honey is our primary sweetener of choice. Honey, taken from high altitudes in the Canadian Rockies is delicious and nutritious. Raw, unprocessed honey is known for its live healing enzymes that can heal skin topically and helps increase one's mental alertness, reflexes and IQ. I would be remiss not mentioning two other amazing super foods as it relates to bees; they are bee pollen and royal jelly. Both are loaded with amazing nutrients and minerals, and when added to your daily diet will help you live longer and feel more alive. However, please don't just take my word for it, go to your local health food store and pick up some today and give it a try!

A discussion on super foods wouldn't be complete without mentioning coconut oil. Coconut oil is one of those rare oils that can be heated to high temperatures without changing its molecular structure. Not only does it taste good but also it's healthy to cook with. However, coconut oil in its raw state is optimal, and David Wolfe says in his book *Superfoods,* "coconut oil consists of 90 + percent raw saturated fat—a rare and important building block of every cell in the human body. Unlike long-chain saturated animal fats, the saturated fat in coconut oil is in the form of medium-chain fatty acids (MCFA's). MCFA's support the immune system, the thyroid gland, the nervous system, skin, and provide for fast energy."

Upon learning this, I immediately switched from drinking Gatorade to coconut water during my workouts, as coconut water is a natural electrolyte and energy-sustaining source.

I could write an entire book on just the topic of super foods; however, David has already done that, so check out his book *Superfoods*, and you'll be amazed with what you learn.

You will find when you start adding super foods and raw foods to your diet and start nourishing your body properly you'll automatically need less food and you won't get hungry. The reason the body gets hungry is because it's seeking nourishment. Hunger is your body's way of saying, "Give me food that I can work with and not foods that are toxic, processed, refined, and genetically modified."

Suffice it to say, super foods are a way to not only nourish your body and brain beyond what you thought possible but also to heal your body of diseases, joint inflammation, and emotional issues such as depression.

A terrific way to get super foods in your body is by adding them to the juice you make from your fruits and vegetables. I recommend following the dosage instructions when it says only start with an ⅛ of a teaspoon and build up from there; it's important to not overwhelm your body even though it's all good for you.

Some people just can't get past starting their day off without a cup of coffee and that's fine; coffee is actually a great base for your super foods shake and can deliver the super foods throughout your body quickly. So make your coffee and use it as a base for your shake if you choose. That being said, limiting caffeine intake is essential to maintaining your energy throughout the day. Other great bases to try for your shakes are almond milk, coconut water, mushroom tea and our all-time favorite, spring water.

When you start adding super foods to your shakes and elixirs you might find the taste is a bit strong, if you do just add cinnamon and more honey. Natural sweeteners are, as I'm sure you guessed, the best way to go. Adding cinnamon to your drinks is a delicious and nutritious way to make your drink more palatable, especially if you venture into adding more super foods and Chinese herbs to your drinks.

One last thing—I use my intuition to guide me as to which super foods need to be in our shakes, and I also go by the colors of the super foods to figure out what a healthy and good tasting combination might be.

For example, when I make our "green" shake I start with almond milk as a base (off-white) then I add chlorella, spirulina, and marine phytoplankton (all of which are green and are quite possibly the healthiest foods you could ever feed your body). Then I add tocotrienols (which has four out of the eight essential vitamin E's and they are white), pearl powder (great for the skin, actually helps you look younger; pearl is white), Lucuma (off-white color and is a healthy sweetener loaded with beta-carotene and iron), and honey. All the colors work together and taste great together.

Water and Its Healing Effects on Your Body

My research into the physical body and its abilities constantly leaves me feeling awestruck. The more I learn about the body and its capabilities the more I believe that thought, consciousness, belief and nutritious foods have far greater impact on our bodies than our genetics.

The human body is made up of 70% to 85% water, and interestingly enough approximately 75% of the Earth's surface is covered in—you guessed it—water. Suffice it to say, water is critical to us and for us. In fact the large battery that powers your body, the brain, is made up of 95% water. Most of the body's oxygen comes from water. Water is absorbed almost immediately in the body and is held within and outside the cells. When your body ages it naturally loses hydration, which causes wrinkles, and that's why it's essential to drink at least eight to ten glasses of water a day. When your body is dehydrated everything slows down. Your thinking, breathing, and ability to focus are affected as well. Consistently drinking mountain spring water throughout the day is essential for you to be well hydrated, and when you're thirsty, that's a sign your body is already dehydrated, meaning you waited too long to drink water.

The best drinking water for your mind, spirit and body is water that is full of minerals and is chemical and toxin free.

Water of this nature is taken directly from a spring at the source and should be stored in glass containers. Check out the site: www.findaspring.com to locate a spring near you. Most of these springs on the site have already been piped and are relatively easy to get to. The fresh water coming from the spring is highly alkaline and can quickly convert excess acid to alkaline within your body, which is another reason to drink lots of spring water. Spring water is the super water of all waters. It's natural and is void of fluoride and other chemicals; it nourishes the brain, carries nutrients and oxygen to your cells, moistens tissue such as mouth and eyes, and helps the body eliminate toxins.

You do *not* want to stop off at any scenic lake or stream by the road and dip your bottle in and start drinking. Many lakes and streams are polluted, so ask around and find a safe water source that you know other people are drinking from too. You can also have water tested at your local community health unit/center, and it's normally free.

As mentioned earlier, your body and your brain are mostly made up of water and your cells are the building blocks of life. Water carries nutrients and oxygen to your cells; the more nourished and oxygenated your cells the less stress on your cells, which helps them live longer and replicate. In turn you'll look and feel younger than your age and your body will be healthy from the inside out, which also helps you live longer. Furthermore, as previously mentioned your body's cells respond to your thoughts, which are kinetic, meaning they are made up of energy and that energy has motion. Water is also kinetic and transmutable meaning it changes form. We see this when water is heated or frozen.

This might be sounding a bit alchemist here, nevertheless, stay with me—this is big! Everything is made up of energy, and therefore vibrates; and everything vibrates at its own unique frequency—including all tangible items such as plants, people, money, houses, cars, and intangibles such as love, happiness, thoughts, and joy.

The vibration or motion of your thoughts affects the water in your body. This in turn affects the frequency with which your body and brain perform and function. To manifest anything you desire (tangible or intangible), all you have to do is focus your crystal clear thoughts or intentions on the spring water you're drinking, and as long as those focused thoughts are based in love, joy, and gratitude you'll magnetize and bring to you anything you desire.

Huge right?

When I came to this conclusion I had to stop writing, drink a glass of water, and allow this amazing information to sink in. Maybe you should do the same.

Some of you might be reading this and thinking did I read that correctly, all I have to do is drink spring water and I can have anything I desire? The answer is both "yes" and "no."

"Yes" because infusing your water with crystal clear intentions based in love and gratitude alerts your brain and body on a cellular level to what you desire to manifest.

"No" because you haven't incorporated the last piece of the puzzle—the spiritual piece that you'll do in the following chapters. Then you'll be set to manifest ANYTHING you desire, no matter how big or small.

Read on.

Masaru Emoto in his groundbreaking book *Messages from Water and the Universe* captured on film water crystal images that changed shape based on the frequency of music, thoughts and phrases the water was exposed to. The most beautiful crystal, in his opinion—and he photographed tens of thousands— is the crystal that was exposed to the phrase "love and gratitude" over a 24-hour period.

Mr. Emoto says, "As a result of much research, I've come to believe that water (taken from a high spring and certainly not tap water) has the capacity to memorize and transfer information, and the photographs of the crystals were proof, confirming that my belief was correct." Mr. Emoto continues, "God created water to help carry out his plans for the universe and in the center of those plans are two important energies: love and gratitude... It can be said that the light of God created the water crystal of love and gratitude. Light is the ultimate creative energy."

Sometimes it's tempting to believe that we must seek out exotic or rare foods to provide us with proper nourishment. Yet the most ubiquitous part of our bodies—natural water from the Earth—can be found in a spring near you. Similarly, I highly suggest shopping for locally grown produce and foods in your geographic area. Farmers' markets are a great way to find amazingly healthy foods and vegetables that taste great and helps support your local community. Think hundred-mile radius when shopping for food and that applies to how far the food has travelled to reach your plate.

Lastly, regarding making healthy choices in terms of food and food preparation. I highly recommend for you to research GMO (genetically modified foods) and microwaves and see if they support you in your quest for true success.

❋ SELF-ASSESSMENT

- Your physical body is mostly water. So it stands to reason that the quality of the water that you put into your body matters. But it's not just the chemical makeup that matters— the minerals and purity—it's also the energy that you put into your water. Water can have positive or negative energy. Whatever energy the water contains goes straight into your body.

- What kinds of energy are you most often infusing your body with?

◆ Pour yourself a nice glass of cool spring water. Take a minute to focus your attention on the water. Fill it with positive energy. Make the water a messenger of love to each and every cell in your body. Empower the water to cleanse your body of toxins.

◆ And above all, thank the water for performing this vital function. Enjoy!

Part III

Reignite Your Fire:
Spirit

Chapter 13:
Ignite Your Spirit

*"Everyone who is seriously involved in the pursuit of
science becomes convinced that a spirit is manifest in
the laws of the Universe—a spirit vastly superior to
that of man, and one in the face of which we with our
modest powers must feel humble."* ~ Albert Einstein

Just as your mind resides in your brain, your spirit resides in
your heart, or more specifically in your heart chakra. Your heart
chakra is located just to the right of your physical heart and is
located in the center of your chest. Chakra's can be thought of as
energy vortexes located throughout your body. I won't discuss
chakras in too much detail here; however, they do help facilitate
the body—spirit connection.

Your spirit is the invisible part of you that tethers you (like
an umbilical cord) to both the universe and to the spiritual realm.
That is why I said at the outset of this book, aligning with your
spirit allows for a recollection of your connection to the
universe. When the connection between your mind, body, and
spirit is made, your inner knowing is enhanced showing you
what is truth and what isn't. Think for a moment in your life,

how many times have you just known the truth about something regardless of what others were saying? Maybe you used words such as, "I'm not sure how I know, I just know." If you ever wondered how you knew something to be true, this is the "how": Your spirit communicated with you via sensations in your body and this happens all the time whether you know it or not.

This inner knowing is foolproof and is there to serve as a guide, pointing out what you need to know at just the right time. Think back to the time you met your spouse or significant other. How did you feel about that person when you met? Can you remember feeling deep inside you that he or she was the right person for you? Sure, some people say, "Yes, I had that feeling—but we ended up getting a divorce." That's okay too; it simply means your journey as a couple was meant to end and another was to begin.

Or perhaps you can think back to a time when an idea dropped in that felt right to you, and upon pursuit of that idea it turned into a successful business. The applications are endless for this knowledge that brings about resonance within you.

Often people use the terms "soul" and "spirit" interchangeably, yet the truth is they are different and have differing roles. You have both a soul and a spirit, and it's impossible to have one without the other. Though they function differently within you, they share a commonality- each connects you to source and guides you, so you can stay connected to your true, authentic self. Some refer to this process of connecting to their authentic self as being guided by a "moral compass."

As previously mentioned, soul and spirit are not the same, and each plays a distinct function or role in your life. To help you understand the difference between the two, bring to mind a car. Your physical body being the actual vehicle while your soul is the driver of the vehicle, and your spirit is the gas that makes the vehicle go. Let's explore each further.

Your Soul

Your soul is subtle, quiet, and patient, and can be thought of as a wise elder who sits and listens attentively to your every word and watches your every action without judgment. Your soul is the observer that overlays your physical body and links you to your source, which is pure perfection. Every soul is the same age, and there is no such thing as an "old soul" or "new soul." However, there are soul levels, and depending on one's awareness and growth via lessons, challenges, struggles, perceived setbacks and failures, one's soul level can vary.

Your soul is here to grow and guide you, and in order to grow you need to be firmly in the game called life, experiencing everything you possibly can, including feeling vulnerable and getting out of your comfort zone. Your soul doesn't want you sitting passively as life goes by, living by someone else's rules or not challenging yourself. No, it wants you out and about, meeting new people, loving and living more deeply, being of service, contributing to society, and healing whatever it is that holds you back.

Before I get into how to ignite your spirit I would like to speak to what people refer to most often as it relates to their soul, and that is their *soul's purpose.*

You have a purpose on this Earth that's designed specifically for you, and it's exactly what you agreed to before you incarnated on this physical Earth plane. For some people that answer is disappointing, because they were hoping for a giant billboard dropping from the sky telling them exactly what they're here to do. However, for others this response is a relief. You chose your life's purpose, lessons, challenges, and obstacles before you came into this Earth school, and your soul is with you to keep you connected to God so you don't get lost.

> *Your soul's purpose can be found where passion and joy intersect in your life.*

Your soul doesn't have an agenda different than what your heart already desires, and that should be a relief. In order to discover your purpose you won't need to implore the universe to tell you what it is. The truth is, your purpose is what you *say* it is. Furthermore, discovering your purpose has a lot to do with what you're most passionate about and what you really enjoy.

However, living your soul's purpose takes courage and is truly the hero's journey since you'll need to summon all of your inner resources to help calm your nerves and quiet your inner critic. If you're able to do so, you'll discover the reason that you're here on Earth, and perhaps for the first time you'll clearly see your role in making the world a better place.

If you're reading this and thinking to yourself that you have no clue what your purpose is, that's okay. Not everyone knows what their soul's purpose is early on in life; in fact, for most, their soul's purpose isn't revealed until they're in their mid forties. I don't know why that is exactly; however, I think it has something to do with that being the approximate age when most people know themselves better—including what they truly enjoy, what they really, really, really desire, and what makes their heart sing. Plus, by that age most people are emotionally mature enough to know there is more to life than just making piles of money and having material possessions. They understand at a deeper level their true value and how they can contribute to society. Most people at that age or older have lived long enough and are truly ready to make changes.

Jimmy Page, guitarist for Led Zeppelin and two-time inductee to the Rock and Roll Hall of Fame, says this about discovering his soul's purpose: "Whether I took it on or it took me on I don't know, the jury is out on that at the moment but I don't care—I've just really, really, really enjoyed it."

I promise you this: your purpose will have nothing to do with what you *don't* enjoy doing. Only the egoistic, conscious thinking mind creates scenarios like that. Your soul's purpose is a way for you to contribute to the greater good, which will fill your soul with joy and passion as your purpose unfolds. Clues to your purpose can be found in those things that bring you pleasure and joy. Some even refer to their purpose as the very thing they would do for free. Furthermore, your purpose includes your inner gifts and the lessons you need to learn during this lifetime. For example, if your lesson this time around has to do with relationships, you might be drawn to become a relationship counselor, yet at the same time you might struggle with your own relationship. Many operate from this dynamic when they utter the words, "Do as I say, not as I do."

The lessons we need to learn and master during this lifetime often bring us to our purpose. Your soul's purpose is a subset of one or several broad categories which are: teacher, parent, healer, artist, laborer, leader, caretaker, student, helper, public servant, rule maker, activist, athlete, or business person.

The next step is to pick from the above-mentioned categories as they relate to your particular passion. For example, if you are passionate about helping people, then you could choose any of the above categories. The way to narrow the playing field is to figure out specific aspects of you, such as, do you enjoy being creative? Do you enjoy being around people? Do you enjoy taking care of others when they are not well? Or perhaps you enjoy working from home? Since each broad category has many subcategories, your answers to those questions will help you hone in on a specific area that you are drawn to. The key in the narrowing process to discover your purpose is to go with *what you enjoy doing most*, not with what makes you most comfortable. Many make the mistake of thinking they are feeding their soul by being comfortable or complacent, and this is furthest from the truth.

The process of discovering your soul's purpose could unfold like this: Main categories that resonate with you are *leader* and *public servant*. While drilling down to the next level you determine you enjoy higher education and helping out the underdog, plus you have a fierce inner drive to see justice served. Knowing this about yourself, you might feel drawn to attend law school, and then after school serve as a public defender. Another example is that you might be drawn to the main categories of teacher, healer, and businessperson. At quick glance, some might say these three categories are unrelated. However, upon exploring your inner desires you find that you have a gift of healing others and you also feel a stirring deep within to help as many people as possible. Your soul's purpose might unfold in such a way that you use your business acumen to serve many people in the process of healing.

The key to determining your soul's purpose is to *trust* in yourself and what you feel drawn to. Furthermore, you nourish your soul by getting out of your comfort zone and by expressing your true self.

Bring to mind Barbara Streisand. It is well known she has had stage fright, yet her voice is certainly a gift she was born with. Now, imagine if she never got past her stage fright and instead chose to live a more quiet and "comfortable" life, never reaching beyond her comfort zone. The world would surely have missed the gifts she gave by her singing and acting.

To discover your soul's purpose, consider aspects that make you unique, where your passion lies, and the lessons you need to learn. These will all help reveal your purpose to you.

Furthermore, your soul's purpose can be found where joy and passion intersect, and it's through your heart and spirit that you align with what brings you joy. That is your purpose—no more and no less. Some experience joy through teaching, leading, acting, singing, song writing, painting, gardening, cooking, writing, or exercising. No matter what it is, if you create a life around what brings you joy, your days will be more purposeful than you can imagine.

> *Self-expression leads to soul-expansion.*

Please do your best to not get caught up in *how* something is going to happen. Just take action daily and watch your purpose unfold. When you take a step toward your purpose unfolding the next step will be revealed. After you take that next step, pause and allow for another step to be revealed, and soon you will be living your purpose.

✳ EXERCISE: "SOUL SPEAK"

With paper and pen, write these words:

What truly brings me joy?

Reflect deeply within and then write what comes.

Your Spirit

Your spirit comprises your personality, likes, and dislikes, and is essentially "you." Spirit is the direct link between you and your soul, and is the part of you that offers gentle nudges and support as you walk along your path in life. As previously mentioned, spirit is the energy that allows your body—your "vehicle"—to go, and it is the breath of life to your physical body. Some people, who have had the privilege of being with someone when they take their last breath and graduate to the spiritual realm, have *felt* the person's spirit exit the body, while others have *seen* the person's spirit leave the body. Your spirit is your personality wielding free will, helping you successfully navigate the choppy waters of life, and assisting you to change and grow.

I personally know that we are much more than our physical bodies. Several years ago I had the experience of leaving my physical body. During that time I was working with the idea of being able to leave my physical body—not to graduate to the spiritual realm but just to have the experience of leaving it for a bit. One night while I was sleeping, I woke up and saw a brilliant white light coming from my hallway. I was curious and wanted to see where the light was coming from, especially since I knew the light wasn't on when I went to sleep. The next thought I had was to get out of bed, however, I soon found myself not using my physical body to get out of bed; rather, I felt myself leave my body through my chest.

At first attempt I didn't leave my body because I hit some type of barrier that didn't allow me to leave. However, on my next attempt I left easily and effortlessly through my chest and soon I found myself floating in the air toward my open door leading to the hallway. As I floated toward the door, I took inventory of my senses and realized I had all of them: even though I wasn't in my body I could see, hear, think, feel, and know. My conscious thinking mind, my ability to reason, and my personality were intact. I even gained the ability to move by using my thoughts rather than my legs. It was as if "I" was all there except for my body. However, the moment I reached the doorway I had the conscious thought "This is so cool, I've left my body," which instantly sent me back to my physical body.

As I lay there in bed, I thought, "Note to self: the next time you leave your body, don't think."

In the very next moment, I saw a figure in a black cloak come out of the white light and into my room. I observed the figure float past the foot of my bed and toward the other side of my bed. Even though I had no idea who was coming toward me, during this entire incident I felt peaceful and not fearful. As the cloaked figure got closer and leaned onto my bed I saw a woman's white slender arm reaching out of her black cloak to lean on. The closer she got to me the more her physical body was revealed. Soon she removed her black hood and I saw her beautiful silky white skin, blue eyes, red lips, and long curly blonde hair. Her beauty was awe inspiring, yet it was her eyes that were most captivating. Her eyes were sparkling and gentle, wise and all knowing.

Next, she communicated to me through thought, and she must have asked if she could kiss me, because I found myself blurting out, "Heck yeah—you're hot." She smiled and leaned in to kiss me. Feeling her lips pressed to mine, I breathed in deeply, and in that moment I woke up.

I know what I experienced was real and not just a dream. I will never forget that incident as long as I live. I feel truly blessed to have been kissed by an angel and whenever I need comforting or reassuring I close my eyes and remember that time and how easy it was to leave my body and how beautiful it was to be kissed by an angel. That experience helped me know for certain that we are much more than just our physical bodies.

The very last words my twin brother said upon his passing verified this knowing that we are much more than our physical bodies. Upon taking his last breath he said, "The people are coming, f**k it, I'm checking out now." He described leaving his body simply by saying, I'm checking out now. I have also come to learn when Steve Jobs passed, his sister reported his last words were, "Oh wow, oh wow, oh wow."

My brother gave me a beautiful gift by narrating his graduation from the physical Earth plane, and I'm happy to share it with you. For me, I have complete comfort in knowing the process most refer to as "dying" and what I refer to as "graduating" is beautiful, joyful, and easy. Truth is, leaving this Earth school is so much easier than staying, and throughout my life I have found that most people who are afraid of "dying" are actually afraid of living.

The human spirit is a variable that can't be measured or quantified. It's the greatest mystery of our world, and our most powerful and essential asset to success and growth. As a recent General Electric commercial said so aptly, "We know much about the human body and know very little about the human spirit." The human spirit is a shifting force that can make an underdog victorious. The spirit allows the defeated to rise back up and try again. Spirit-driven people feel passion and purpose beyond what most only dream of, making them VIPs in the game of life. Such people move forward in life, past all perceived obstacles, welcoming challenges that come their way.

For those conscious and awake people, you'll want to spend lots of time discovering who you truly are in terms of what motivates you, inspires you, and what ignites your spirit and sets it ablaze with passion.

Everyone can access their inner core. They just need to know how—so let's get started. Tapping into your spirit requires you to take the longest 16-inch journey of your life, from your head (which is the location of your conscious-thinking mind) to your heart (which is the center of your feelings). Only the willing person who is truly ready for change will be interested in such a journey. It may sound like a simple line to walk, being such a short distance, but in truth the path is often wrought with fear, self-doubt and confusion. The fact that so much importance exists in this realm adds weight to the great mystery of the spirit. Surrendering and releasing control is essential for moving from your head to your heart, making it no easy task. However, if you're determined to succeed, and allow yourself to stay the course, it'll be the most rewarding journey of your life.

Why get out of your head and operate from your heart? Because of one word: emotions. Emotions fuel the fire of your spirit and your spirit stokes the fire of your soul. Without emotions and feelings you can't get your life party started! Enthusiasm and passion are the precursors to joy, and as you already know, that is where your purpose lies.

Bring to mind someone aligned with his or her purpose. They are probably quite enthusiastic, passionate, and up beat. They seem to know a secret that others can't quite figure out. The truth is there is no secret; the only thing they know that others don't is that they live with passion and enthusiasm every day by choice, not by chance. They *choose* to feel alive and energetic and these powerful feelings go out into the universe and bring them opportunities to expand their life and their success. They know they alone are responsible for creating their success. They believe in a philosophy that holds true regarding everything, and that is: a body at rest stays at rest, a body in motion stays in motion. They choose motion, and their motion produces productivity and creates a spirit that is alive and on fire!

Many people wait. They wait to feel inspired and passionate, and to that I say you are going to wait a long time. You need to fuel your spirit—that's the only way to ignite it. *Set your spirit ablaze by choice, not circumstance, and your life will be forever changed.*

Developing Your Inner Knowing

Knowing your soul's purpose and living it is a significant step on the path of true success. I believe life is God's gift to us and our gift to God is what we make of our life. However, taking hold of the "reins" in life and stepping into your purpose with passion can be scary. If you had a way of knowing for certain you were making the right decision, would your journey be less challenging? What if you had a way to tell instantly if someone was trustworthy or not? What if you had the ability to know something was going to happen before it did? What if you knew for certain whether or not making a potential investment would yield positive results *before* you made it?

Well, guess what: you do have the ability to know all that and much more! And I'm here to help you develop those abilities.

As I said earlier, everyone has an intuitive side, and it's often referred to as intuition, gut feelings, an inner knowing, or sixth sense. It doesn't really matter what you call it, just know you already possess it. This is a tool you were born with, and frankly it's one of the most powerful—yet underutilized—tools most people have. Your intuition is your ability to see into yourself and to know things about yourself and what resonates with you, which is different than being psychic.

A psychic is someone who has developed their ability to receive information about others. When psychics are in tune with their client they can provide information to them regarding their relationships, finances, health, business deals, and anything else the client wants to know.

While I believe everyone has psychic abilities, that's not what this book is about.

Your Intuition

*"Intuition is a spiritual faculty and does not explain,
but simply points the way."* ~ Florence Scovel Shinn

You can achieve anything you desire and reduce the time it takes to become successful by developing and following your inner guidance. Everything about tapping into your inner guidance or "sixth sense" is simple; the challenge comes in getting you to believe that you *have* a sixth sense, and then getting you to *follow* your inner guidance.

Your sixth sense is your internal feedback mechanism that communicates information to you through your traditional five senses plus through hunches, twinges, heart flutters, goose bumps, gut feelings, and mutual pings (the thing that happens when two people think of each other simultaneously). Your sixth sense also communicates with you by showing you pictures in your mind (via your pineal gland), by way of inspired thoughts, and by sharing information via dreams and visions.

What type of information does it communicate, you ask? It will communicate basically anything you want to know and then some. Your sixth sense is a mechanism designed to seek the truth and communicate that truth to you regarding every situation in your life.

Think back to a time when you knew for certain an event was going to happen and then it did. Perhaps you were thinking of a friend and all of a sudden the phone rang and they were on the other end of the line. Maybe you were working through an idea for your business and an inspired thought instantly dropped into your mind and brought you the answer you needed. Perhaps your relationship was confusing you, and then a song on the radio resonated with you and helped you figure out a solution to your challenge.

From these examples you might think, well, the information just came out of the blue. To which I say, exactly! Your job is to be clear about what it is you need assistance with and then put it out into the universe. I share exactly how that works in the next chapter called "The Golden Grid."

Okay, so after you put out into the universe what you desire, you next step is to *wait*. Yes, I said wait, or more specifically be aware of what comes to you in the form of signs such as inspired thoughts, vivid dreams, a song on the radio, a blog on the internet, a phone call "out of the blue"—the list goes on and on.

Once you receive the sign, take action. It's really that simple.

I'll give you a funny example of a sign from the universe. The brother of a friend of mine had graduated to the spiritual realm, or as some say, had passed on. My friend was really struggling with his passing and was desperately looking for a sign that her brother was okay. One morning she went out for a run and as she walked out the front door, a bird pooped right on her head. She laughed and knew it was a sign from her brother. Maybe asking for a less messy sign is a good idea. If you've received signs from the universe in funny or unique ways, please email me at jaden@jadensterling.com and let me know. I would love to hear about them.

As previously mentioned, in order to get your attention the universe can show you signs in many ways. Your sixth sense, however, can be subtler, which is why most overlook its value and some never even acknowledge its existence. Your sixth sense communicates a message to you every time someone "rubs you the wrong way," or when you have an uneasy feeling in your gut, or when you know something isn't quite right about a situation but you "just can't put your finger on it," or when you meet your life partner and you just know the two of you are going to be together, or when you're interviewing someone for a job and you know they're the right fit the moment you met. All of these are examples of communication received directly from your sixth sense. Your sixth sense is foolproof, yet it's also the most underutilized sense people have.

A few really successful people who routinely followed their inner guidance are Tom Ford, Anne Lamott and Steven Jobs. The following is/was their process of tapping into their intuition to reach their creative self.

Tom Ford, the famed designer for Gucci and Yves Saint Laurent and an Oscar-nominated movie producer, describes the start of his creative process is when he stops thinking and starts feeling. Tom says, "There are no right or wrong answers; it's intuition." Tom says his biggest and best ideas come when he has moments of clarity and when silence drowns out noise so that he can feel rather than think.

Anne Lamott, *multiple New York Times* bestselling author says, "I had to stop living unconsciously, as if I had all the time in the world. The love and good and the wild and the peace and creation that are you will reveal themselves, but it is harder when they have to catch up to you in roadrunner mode. So one day I did stop. I began consciously to break the rules I learned in childhood: I wasted more time, as a radical act. I stared off into space more, into the middle distance, like a cat. This is when I have my best ideas, my deepest insights."

The late, Steven Jobs (founder of Apple) said, "Your time is limited, so don't waste it living someone else's life. Don't be trapped by dogma, which is living with the results of other people's thinking. Don't let the noise of other's opinions drown out your own inner voice. And most important, have the courage to follow your heart and intuition they somehow already know what you truly want to become. Everything else is secondary. This approach has never let me down, and it has made all the difference in my life."

> *Be true to yourself and breathe life into the thing inside of you that wants to express itself, take root, and see the light of day.*

This is a plain and simple truth to live by: don't let other people tell you what you can and cannot do.

Early on, I started recognizing that my sixth sense was communicating information to me when I uttered the words, "I wonder if..." After years of saying, "I wonder if ..." I began to notice that the very thing I wondered about always happened. I soon realized that by thinking "I wonder if...," I was actually receiving a clue about something that would happen in the very near future. "I wonder if ..." came to me regarding stocks, too, by thinking, "I wonder if XYZ Company is going to be bought out?" Sure enough, within a few days it would be! Over time, I trained myself to pay closer attention when my inner dialogue started with, "I wonder if ..."

Another way guidance comes is in the form of your senses (hearing, seeing, feeling, and knowing). Your intuitive senses can be thought of as heightened physical senses. Some people may receive information through some or all of their heightened senses. Those who are more visual receive images or pictures and do so in their mind's eye (pineal gland). Some people are auditory and will hear guidance that comes in the form of their own voice and that offers helpful ideas, suggestions, or clues to solve a problem. Others might receive thoughts or ideas that "drop in" allowing them to *know* information. Then there are people who receive guidance through their physical bodies in terms of feelings. Gut feelings are one way, and because the digestive tract actually has an intricate network of neurons that relay messages to our large brain, scientists have called this the "second brain" (Hadhazy 2010). This second brain is often the reason people have such strong gut feelings that can't be ignored.

After discovering how guidance comes to you, the next step is to discipline yourself to follow through on the guidance you receive. This is the most challenging part for people because often they don't trust they are receiving amazingly accurate information. To that I say, just give it a try and see what happens. You don't have to take action regarding every little bit of guidance from the universe, but what would happen if you started acting on, let's say, half of it for now? What do you have to lose—or more aptly, what would you gain?

In *Think and Grow Rich* by Napoleon Hill, which I've read a dozen times, the sixth sense is mentioned repeatedly. Hill says, "I find my mind most receptive to ideas, thoughts, and knowledge which reach me through the sixth sense." Furthermore, he writes, the "sixth sense is the faculty which marks the difference between a genius and an ordinary individual." I believe he and I are referring to the same thing. Napoleon Hill attributes the sixth sense to helping ordinary people become extraordinary, to which I say a resounding "Yes!"

Your life will change immeasurably when you start to trust and act on the information that you receive. Following guidance from your intuition or sixth sense will make your life easier, more joyful, more productive, and enriched. I utilize my sixth sense to help me pick the right stocks to buy and show me the right sectors at just the right time, and my portfolio returns are consistently higher than the market averages year over year.

The other neat thing is, the more you act on the information you receive the more information you'll get.

Your sixth sense, simply put, is the mechanism for which you receive guidance and information from your higher self. When followed, it will allow your life to unfold easily, blissfully and successfully.

Now I am going to share with you a secret—well, I guess it's not a secret anymore but it's something amazing I recently learned from my guides and master teachers from the spiritual realm—about how you can use the power of your mind, body and spirit to connect with the universe to achieve anything you desire. The secret is found in the next chapter. However, please don't skip ahead—remember to do the self-assessment on the next page.

✻ SELF-ASSESSMENT

- Is there an area in your life for which you seek clarification? If so, what is it and have you asked the universe for help?

- Have you taken some time to still your mind and to receive the guidance the universe has for you?

- Now, after asking the universe, are you ready to follow through with the guidance the universe brings?

- If not, what stops you from trusting and acting upon this guidance?

Chapter 14:
The Golden Grid:
How to Manifest Anything

"Neo, sooner or later you're going to realize, just as I did, that there's a difference between knowing the path, and walking the path."
~ Morpheus, *The Matrix*

You create your reality through your own perception of that which you experience in every moment of every day. Your life is unfolding not by chance or accident but rather deliberately and with assistance from the universe. Some make the conscious choice to be successful during difficult economic times, while others aren't able to achieve a lasting level of success even during prosperous times. Why is it that some are able to rise above the tide and thrive, while others flounder? What is the root cause of our differentiating levels of success, regardless of the current economic climate?

These are the types of questions that I ruminate on when I'm in meditation or when I'm relaxing. I attempt to understand the workings of the world in order to better help others and myself achieve lofty goals. Recently, during one such meditation, I posed that last important question to the universe in a bid to understand just how we create our own reality. I turned the question over in my mind, searching through the ether for solutions.

Suddenly, I was struck with a powerful visualization: I was presented with the vision of a glowing golden grid. The image was laid out above my head and below my feet in an ascending pattern. At first I did not know what the grid signified; however after meditating further and thinking about the message later, the meaning of the grid and its valuable insights for manifesting our experiences became apparent.

I named the system that was presented to me the Golden Grid. Others have seen the grid as well and refer to it as the matrix, holographic field, or source field.

The Golden Grid is above your head and below your feet and connects everything and everyone in the universe to each other. It's invisible to your physical eyes, but it can be seen by your third eye. You might find it helpful to think of the Golden Grid as you would the Internet, a way to connect everyone, yet no one really knows how or where the connection takes place. Personally, I think the Golden Grid is the very reason everyone is connected via the Internet. However, unlike the Internet the Golden Grid always delivers and never stops working so you'll never receive an error message such as, "network lost" that can appear on your wireless devices.

Here's how the grid works. Your life experiences are woven together by threads called your thoughts, beliefs, feelings, and actions or inactions. You are presented choices every second of the day, and you are responsible for choosing the ways in which to think, to feel and to believe. This applies to the interactions that you have in regards to every person, place, and thing that you encounter throughout your entire life. Your thoughts, feelings and actions align you along the scaling system of the Golden Grid, which without fail gives you in return a corresponding vibrational match to that which you send out.

It might be helpful for you to think of your thoughts and feelings as boomerangs bringing back to you a vibrational match of what you put out into the world.

In other words:

> *You're the initiator and creator of your experiences because of the energy and vibration that you extend out and into the universe.*

Really, it's that simple; and if you desire to change your experience in life then simply change what you send out onto the grid via your thoughts, actions, and feelings, and you'll create an entirely new experience.

To fully understand how to manifest anything via the Golden Grid it is important to consider the variety of thoughts you have on any given day. Your thoughts can be grouped primarily into one of two categories, which are: complete or incomplete. The thoughts that connect onto the Golden Grid are those that are complete rather than incomplete. Incomplete thoughts lack power, are fleeting, and don't resonate or interest you enough for you to follow through with them. Consider for a moment your mental chatter, and you (along with everyone else) will have plenty examples of incomplete thoughts.

On the contrary, a complete thought is a thought that is well formed, focused, and concentrated. Complete thoughts are organized, specific, identifiable (understood) and quantifiable (measured). A complete thought is similar to setting an intention that focuses on a clear end result. Complete thoughts are powerful and "weighty" and give rise to your spirit and its desires.

Prayer is a complete thought. A prayer that is said repeatedly and with earnest connects to the Golden Grid.

Actions are similar to thoughts, in that inconsistent action or inaction has little connectivity to the grid. However, action taken consistently and repeatedly with the intention of being of service to others connects directly on the grid.

This connection to the grid works similarly to plugging in a lamp into an electrical socket. The lamp must be plugged into some type of power source (electrical, battery or solar) for it to work. People are designed the same way, in that we must be plugged into our source (higher power) for us to shine our bright light and to perform our very best.

Lastly are feelings. As previously mentioned, the feelings you emit from your heart have been measured to extend approximately two kilometers from your body. Feelings of love, joy and gratitude are the most powerful feelings available to you on this planet (and I suspect on other planets as well). Allowing yourself to feel joy, love, and gratitude strongly connects you to the Golden Grid faster than the speed of light and amplifies your connection.

There you have it!

> *Your complete thoughts and consistent action fueled by feelings of love, joy, and gratitude help you manifest anything your heart desires via The Golden Grid!*

Levels Of The Grid

There are infinite levels of the grid, however my guides have shown me seven levels to discuss in this book. Each level has a corresponding attribute. These levels are intended as guidelines, since many more experiences exist beyond what is presented below. Furthermore, each level on the grid has a corresponding frequency or vibration attached to it. Your experiences change when you move between the levels of the grid by raising or lowering your frequency of thought, action or belief. Each step up the grid improves the quality of your life and increases the likelihood of you living a life of true success. The seven main attributes of the Golden Grid are:

7. Faith (highest frequency)

6. Trust

5. Cooperation

4. Compassion

3. Empathy

2. Judgment

1. Fear (lowest frequency)

The vibrations of the Golden Grid act as a magnet, drawing to you exactly what you project.

1. *Fear* is, of course, the lowest level on the Golden Grid. This is due to the fact that when you allow fearful thoughts to dominate your perceptions, your vibration will be lowered, which connects you to the lowest level on the grid. Your fearful thinking will return to you the lowest frequency from others as well, bringing the experience of lack, worry, limitation, and more reasons to continue feeling afraid.

I'll give you an example. My wife and I were driving through the mountain range along Kootenay parkway in British Columbia one winter. I had come from Florida and had limited experience driving on winter roads. Although the roads were frequently plowed, the snowplow trucks left behind gravel. If you've spent any time in Canada you'll more than likely see lots of vehicles with cracks in their windshield, and that's because the gravel chunks that get left behind by snowplow trucks become mini projectiles capable of cracking windshields upon impact. The most common way gravel comes in contact with a windshield is via other vehicles' tires, especially the rear ones if you're following too closely.

As I said, it was my first winter driving in Canada and my wife repeatedly told me not to follow too closely behind other vehicles and to allow for lots of space between our vehicle and others if I wanted to pass. I was driving her car, which was only eight months old at the time and had an unblemished windshield. Needless to say, I was a nervous wreck, and prior to her bringing to my attention the potential hazard of rocks hitting the windshield the thought (fear) never entered my mind. My fear forced me to slow down and allow for plenty of room between my car and the vehicle in front of me; however, within a few minutes a truck going in the opposite direction passed us and a rock from its tire hit our windshield and chipped it. I manifested exactly what I was fearful of and did so almost instantaneously.

Perhaps you can recall a time when your feelings of fear brought you more experiences to keep you feeling afraid, thus perpetuating the cycle.

2. Similarly, when you're projecting vibrations of *Judgment* into the universe, you will in turn attract people, places and things that are vibrating at a similar frequency. By your judging others, it's possible that others may gossip about you, avoid you,

and this will surely lead to a pattern of self-judgment that can erupt within your own being. The quickest and most effective way to heal judgment, fear and all forms of negativity is to ask the universe to remove judgment from your heart and keep asking until it's removed.

3. The next level on the Golden Grid is the energy that's aligned with *Empathy*. If you're persistently projecting empathy into the universe, you're positively aligning with the desire to sincerely understand others, and to relate to the challenges or success that they are experiencing themselves. This level of resonating in return will attract positivity to you, manifesting itself in the form of people who can relate to your own particular needs and desires, and may even be able to assist you along your path. Forming a community of empathetic support is incredibly useful along your path to true success. Surrounding yourself with others vibrating on a similar frequency will help to jump start positive results.

4. After you have successfully learned to relate to others and treat them with patience and an open mind, you'll be in an excellent position to feel *Compassion* toward others as well. Compassion, when expressed outwardly for other people, places and things, can energetically align your vibrations with the powerful experience of inner peace. The experience of inner peace will leave you feeling calm, relaxed, and in the perfect space to experience deep satisfaction with your life.

5. The next level on the grid is the experience of unity that comes when you're able to successfully cooperate and partner with others. *Cooperation* and teambuilding with others allows you to build strong synergistic relationships, bringing to you the experience of true success faster. Once you have mastered cooperation, you can begin to accelerate upward and into trust.

6. *Trust* is indispensable to wholeness and is a precursor to knowing. Trusting in one's self and in the universe allows for you to know for certain you can manifest most anything in life. Being able to release and allow others to do their share, while trusting that the universe will provide, raises the human frequency vibration to a very high level. When you align with a very high vibration on the Golden Grid such as the energy of trust, you can expect to experience people, places and things that are aligned with harmonious energy. Harmony comes when you trust that everything is working for your highest and best outcome, and that it always will. Trust and fear are not compatible frequencies; and being aware and stopping yourself when you dip to lower levels on the grid is essential to your progress. To trust is a verb, and is expressed not only when you have all the answers but also when you don't have all the answers.

7. The very highest level on the Golden Grid is *Faith*. Faith is the twin of trust. Faith and fear cannot coexist, and at all times you're operating out of either fear or faith and never both at the

same time, because they are contrary elements. When you project feelings out into the universe, thoughts and actions based in faith are aligned with the highest vibration that exists.

Faith does not have to be couched in a particular religion. It's merely a step beyond trust that means giving yourself over to the universe and believing in a positive result for your future, along with your good intentions. Aligning with the vibration of faith allows you to be of service to others, and to partake in inspired action. Doing so will bring you love, success, joy, gratitude and all the blessings your heart desires!

Below is a table summarizing the kinds of experiences you can expect to receive based on the energy you send out.

Grid Level	Send Out	Receive
7	Faith	Blessings
6	Trust	Harmony
5	Cooperation	Unity
4	Compassion	Peace
3	Empathy	Assistance
2	Judgment	Pain
1	Fear	Lack

Being in Service

If you're searching for a way within the Golden Grid to reach the top at a faster rate, I suggest that you focus your intentions on being of service. When you're acting in service to others, your community and the planet will bring you the greatest rewards. Your joyful, happy, positive thoughts and good deeds will be sent out into the universe at the highest level on the Golden Grid, and will connect with others who are also on the same level. Your good intentions will be amplified and rewarded with support in whatever form you need from the universe.

Simply put, this is the way in which you can attract happy customers, clients, and everything that's aligned with the highest vibrational energy in the universe.

An example of this recently appeared in the news. On a chilly Winnipeg morning, bus driver Kris Doubledee did something he didn't even have to think about and something he said he'd do a thousand times over. He stopped his bus, took his shoes off, and gave them to a barefoot man who may have been homeless. The driver had noticed the barefoot man the day before, but on the second day was in a position to help. His kindness now has his phone ringing off the hook and he appeared on the *CBS This Morning* show in New York City. Doubledee just hopes his story inspires others to perform similar acts.

Are you aware of how challenging it is to get on CBS's This Morning show? Kris didn't have a problem because as the story says they called him. Why? Simple, his actions were aligned with being of service, which connected him to the highest level of the grid.

The Golden Grid is the very reason why your thoughts and feelings are able to produce tangible results. Now that you're aware of the methodology of the Golden Grid, imagine the ways that you can utilize it in your own life for a shift toward true personal success and abundance.

I recorded a short, (free) guided meditation that is available at: www.thewealthquest.com/bookresources the meditation helps you set an intention for the day and to connect onto the grid in order to manifest your intention quickly. Let me know what you think of it, I'd love to hear.

✳ SELF-ASSESSMENT

- ◆ At what level do you feel your thoughts; beliefs and actions most often connect you onto the Golden Grid?

- ◆ What changes would you have to make to your thoughts, beliefs and actions in order to raise the level at which you connect onto the grid?

The next time you meditate and get in touch with your inner self, get clear about what you desire to manifest and focus on where you want to connect onto the grid. One way to do this is to spend time each morning in meditation—five to ten minutes while walking the dog, or preparing breakfast, or right when you wake up before getting out of bed.

Here's what you do: thank the universe for bringing you opportunities to_____ (fill in the blank) that are for your highest and best. You can also ask for very specific things such as the universe to bring you happy new clients, perfect health, a date for later that night, free stuff—it works for anything and everything. Then go about your day as you normally would, trusting and feeling genuinely grateful for the wonderful opportunities that come your way and see what happens. This exercise helps you intentionally manifest experiences that make up your day.

It's a simple formula:

Give with the highest intention to be of service to others, and do so from your heart. Expect nothing in return and the universe will bless you with everything and anything you need.

Chapter 15:
Take Risks – Your Success Depends On It!

"Progress always involves risks. You can't steal
second base and keep your foot on first."
~ Frederick B. Wilcox

When I was in my early 20s I had a friend who told me a story that has forever shaped how I view investment opportunities and taking risks. My friend Moe told me when he was in his 20s (this was in the late 1960s) he loved to surf, and he moved to Hawaii for a year so that he could surf the big waves. While in Hawaii he met two Aussies who also loved to surf and were in Hawaii for the very same reason. Over the summer all three formed a close friendship and when the two Aussies felt they could trust my friend Moe they shared with him their idea: they wanted to start a t-shirt and swimwear company catering to surfers and other water sports enthusiasts. Their biggest challenge was that they needed some seed money to start their business, since all the money they had went to funding their

Hawaii trip. They offered Moe a 10% stake in their company for a $1,000 investment.

Moe thought about it for a while and although he had the money he decided it would be too much of a risk. After all, who would be interested in buying t-shirts and shorts sold by a company called Quiksilver?

My friend Moe "graduated" (passed on) a few years after we met, but I knew him long enough to hear him repeatedly say, "Take risks and trust what's presented to you."

Moe was right. Take risks and trust.

Risk/Reward Ratio

"The greater the reward the greater the risk" does not always hold true. Factors to consider regarding taking potential risks include:

First, carefully analyze and study your risk tolerance and your ability to handle risk, a.k.a. what keeps you up at night.

Second, understand the inherent risk already built into the investment or opportunity in question.

Third, know what opportunity exists in the marketplace for the idea or product you are considering buying, starting, offering, or creating.

Let's examine each. To determine your ability to take risks ask yourself this question: "How comfortable or uncomfortable am I with being wrong, looking foolish or making mistakes?" The answer to these questions will determine your ability to take risks because it's inevitable during your quest for personal freedom and true success that you will experience setbacks and failures. However, the truth is you can fail your way to success (and most do) as long as you look at your journey of failed mishaps as ways to *not* do things and as motivation to learn from and to find a way that will work.

Many great achievers have failed miserably, but they didn't give up or lose faith. They just simply found a new way of accomplishing their goals. Henry Ford is one example; he went broke five times and failed at his early attempts at business before he founded Ford Motor Company. And do you know why the Model T, which was his first great success, was designated "T"? It was because many earlier models, A-S did not sell.

Another example is Walt Disney. A newspaper editor fired him because "he lacked imagination and had no good ideas." After that, Disney started a number of businesses that didn't last and ended up filing bankruptcy. However, Disney kept plugging along, and eventually followed a creative hunch he had while on a train with his wife. An image of a mouse popped in his head and after he quickly sketched it he named him Mortimer. His wife didn't like the name and quickly intervened offering the name Mickey as a suggestion, and the rest is history.

Thomas Edison made a thousand unsuccessful attempts at inventing the light bulb and he was smart enough to learn from each failed attempt.

Oprah Winfrey was fired from a network station as a reporter and told she was "unfit for television."

J.K. Rowling, author of the *Harry Potter* series, started out nearly penniless, severely depressed, divorced, and trying to raise a child on her own while attending school and writing a novel. Rowling spent hours in a warm coffee shop writing with her toddler in a stroller next to her, determined to put down on paper all the imaginings swirling around in her head. Rowling went from being on welfare to being one of the richest women in the world in only five years. I watched an interview with J.K. Rowling that showed her going back to the tiny government subsidized apartment where she was living when she wrote the first novel in the Harry Potter series. She was over taken when she glanced at the person's bookshelf who was currently living there and saw the entire Harry Potter book series on the shelf. Leaning against the wall in tears she kept repeating, "It's so surreal."

I could fill an entire book of stories just like these—stories of people who have worked hard, failed, and then succeeded. It's a no wonder most say it takes eight years to become an overnight success.

Maybe the key to experiencing success is truly to rejoice and be happy when you feel like you "failed," because after failing you really are that much closer to succeeding. Maybe for some you will need to switch businesses, get a new partner, invent a new idea, find additional funding no matter what it is, stay flexible with your footing but firm with your vision.

I remember a time in my professional career when I was buying apartment buildings and converting them into quality affordable housing, and I couldn't find anyone to invest with me. For whatever reason, no one would put up the cash, and when I did find someone to invest they always backed out.

However, I knew several things, all of which I have shared in this book and will list here. First, I knew helping people by offering quality affordable housing was a great thing and I couldn't go wrong, especially since everything in my gut was telling me to go for it.

Next, I believed everything happens *for* me rather than *to* me, so when I couldn't find a partner I figured something else would work out.

Third, I kept moving in the direction of my goal and dream by telling everyone what I was doing and what I needed to make my dream come true. I believed that help and support would come from the universe in some form or another; I just wasn't sure how. This belief kept me attached to the Golden Grid of infinite possibilities.

Lastly, I took my contractor up on an offer to go to a baseball game and to sit in the city's luxury box. There I met the head of the housing department for the city, who asked me what projects I was working on. I told him about the eighteen-unit apartment building I was buying to convert into affordable housing, and he just happened to have a budget to fund projects just like mine.

Magic happens when we trust in the universe and take steps toward fulfilling our goals and dreams.

One last thing about the real estate deal. I bought the building with the help of a zero- interest loan from the city, fixed it up, rented it to people who were living on rent vouchers and public assistance, and sold it eighteen months later. After paying the city back their loan I made over $900,000. When I sold the building I was very happy to not split my check with anyone, and it was then I could see why getting an investor never worked out, thankfully!

Over the last twenty-four years of being a professional real estate investor and stock investor I have learned a few things about risk taking, and I have learned way more from my mistakes than I have my successes. My mistakes have taught me to always, and no matter what, trust my intuition. Whenever I have gone against what my gut told me I have always suffered a loss—financially if it was my professional life, and emotionally if it was my personal life.

Furthermore, I learned to never allow my ego to take over when I'm considering investment opportunities. This mistake cost me $400,000 in cash. I'll spare you the details; just know if you're putting your money where your ego is, eventually you will be in big trouble!

Next, keep your overhead low and your revenue high. Ego can step in again when it comes to having employees, renting office space, advertising, etc. Ego will make you think you need lots of people to work for you and you need to rent the biggest and best office space you can find, and that advertising during the Super Bowl would be a great idea.

Consider when starting or expanding a business to hire subcontractors rather than full time employees. Hiring subcontractors via online companies such as Elance.com or Guru.com can benefit you several ways. First, you'll be searching through a pool of people who are experts in their field and who are already doing the job you're looking to fill, and you don't need to hire them full time. In other words, they're a better fit than your cousin Tom who just needs a job but who really isn't qualified to do what you need done. Another reason why these sites are great is because it forces you to clearly define what the job is that needs accomplishing. Then after you clearly define what needs to be accomplished, providers from all over the world bid on the job. These online services allow you to choose prospective contractors from a much larger pool than you have in your immediate area. Often times you can hire them less expensively, and they're paid when the job is completed to your satisfaction, which doesn't get much better than that. Can you tell I'm a huge advocate of hiring subcontractors online?

The next thing I learned was to not put all my eggs in one basket. I know it sounds like a cliché, doesn't it? It might be a cliché, but it's true! Stay diversified but not overly diversified. What does that mean? It means to figure out your core product and add products or services that, as my good friend Joel says, "stack." In other words, offer additional products or services that are in alignment with your main offering. For instance, Disney started out as a film company, and as that became successful they opened the theme parks and sold Disney apparel and they just kept adding products. The key with additional offerings is to make sure they are related to your main product or your brand. Think outdoor art show, not flea market. Remember the last art show you attended? Did you notice the artists' unique offerings—whether it was through the medium of painting, sculpting, glass blowing, crafting, weaving, carving, or photography—and how their work captured their inner gifts? These artists found their inner calling and offer through art shows and other means a way to add products that are related to their craft.

In addition to staying focused with your offerings know when to cut your losses. As a general rule, if you're continually bumping up against obstacles—and I mean large obstacles—while pursuing your goals and dreams, and this goes on for six months or longer, it may be time to call it quits. I don't mean give up; I mean look for another direction to go in or idea to run with. Generally speaking, ideas that you pursue that come from your higher self are the ones that you're most passionate about and that you know in your heart of hearts you need to follow.

The ones that are founded on lower energy, such as a product or service that is about just making you a lot of money and doesn't really help anyone else should be abandoned quickly. Now, there is nothing wrong with making money, in fact it's great to make money, but it's even better to be of service to others and have a vision that will contribute to the greater good.

Be Productive

Another crucial step for experiencing true success is learning the difference between being productive and being busy. Being busy makes people feel like they are accomplishing tasks simply because they are filling their time. Filling time or having the mindset you have to "put in your time before being successful" is not productive nor is it an efficient use of your time and energy. The key is to know the difference between being productive and being busy.

Being busy can become addictive. When someone calls you and asks how you're doing, most reply by saying, "Good," followed by, "Busy." Think about your own life. How often do you tell people how busy you are?

The key to accomplishing your goals and living your dreams is to replace being *busy* with being *productive*.

I work from home, and initially it was easy for me to get distracted, so I had to learn to behave with self-discipline. I do so by constantly checking in with myself, asking, "Is what I'm doing right now the best possible use of my time?" and "Is this task moving me closer to accomplishing my daily goal?"

Often, people may call or stop by during your workday because they don't have anything else to do. It's easy to get caught up in talking with them. It feels good and it's allowed, perhaps because you don't want to hurt their feelings.

From now on, set boundaries and don't waver. If someone shows up at your door during your workday, try and meet him or her at the door, not letting them in and politely say you'll call them later because you're working. Tell them you're on a deadline for an important client (which you are because the universe is your client and it wants you to be productive and share your gifts)! Being disciplined, honoring your time and setting proper boundaries with others and yourself are the keys to accomplishing your daily goals.

The alternative is unpleasant, since each minute wasted can never be recaptured. Make the best use of your time right now! Time is money, and if you're allowing others to waste your time, then you're also allowing them to take your money.

To further your productivity while working through your daily goals, aim to accomplish early in your day the most difficult task or the one that you have been putting off. This will give you the confidence to tackle your to-do list with vigor. Remember that life is a marathon. If you pace yourself and keep putting one foot in front of the other, you'll accomplish your goals.

Own Your Time

"Until one is committed, there is hesitancy, the chance to draw back - Concerning all acts of initiative (and creation), there is one elementary truth that ignorance of which kills countless ideas and splendid plans: that the moment one definitely commits oneself, then Providence moves too. All sorts of things occur to help one that would never otherwise have occurred. A whole stream of events issues from the decision, raising in one's favor all manner of unforeseen incidents and meetings and material assistance, which no man could have dreamed would have come his way. Whatever you can do, or dream you can, begin it. Boldness has genius, power, and magic in it. Begin it now."

~ Goethe

In order for your dreams to see the light of day you must take daily action. Action taken consistently and repeatedly will bring your dreams to life. I've already talked about the type of action to take and that is, *inspired action*. Inspired action is taking action in the direction that feels best to you. Next, you might find it helpful to create a system for managing the element we call *time*.

Our system of time allows for tremendous acts of creation or busyness, and it's completely up to you which occurs. Regardless of what you do with your time, whether you spend it, waste it, invest it or try to manage it, you will never get it back.

227

That is why it's important to make the best use of the present moment and you do so, by being fully present. Notice I didn't say be productive every moment of the day, I just said be fully present. Whether you are goofing off, making love, working, playing with your kids, exercising, or hanging out with friends, be present so that you can (as my step-up-son says) "juice" the moment. When you fully show up for life, and make a concerted effort to be balanced, nothing and no one in your life will suffer—especially you. To accomplish this you will need to allot time each day to nourish your mind, body and spirit. At this point in the book, I am sure you understand being balanced and present is the basis of true success and the ultimate outcome is for you to have joy, happiness and peace in your life.

That being said, what most people fail to realize when it comes to achieving balance is, you have to be really disciplined and focused with your time and energy. Here are a few techniques I have used for decades to help me achieve balance and be productive.

Create your to-do list for the following day, the night before. Your to-do list should include three main projects and no more than two small projects. This accomplishes a few things.

First, you will sleep better because you were able to clear your mind of work.

Secondly, you will arrive at your place of work knowing exactly what you want to accomplish that day. If you wait for morning to write your daily goals, you will find it is easy to lose focus and become scattered.

Next, when it comes to your projects focus on quality rather than quantity. A lot of my coaching clients who first come to me tell me their biggest obstacle they have is, time. Specifically, finding the time for the important things they really want to accomplish. I then ask about their current daily schedule or plan and 90% don't have one. The reality hits them that they just haven't made their projects a priority. Most realize time isn't really a problem; the problem is they don't have a systematic way to accomplish their goals. And many have bought into the erroneous belief that multi-tasking is the way to get ahead. However, trying to do too much in a day will leave you feeling frustrated and at the end of the day few things get accomplished and those that do aren't done well.

How do you create a systematic plan you ask?

Simple, choose three things to accomplish each day that are measureable or quantifiable and then work in what I call "Power Segments".

Power Segments are *uninterrupted* ninety-minute chunks of time that allow you to be more productive and focused and to work without distractions. For you to not be distracted you might need to: turn off your phone, close your computer browser, and put a "do not disturb" sign on your door. Whatever it takes for you to have uninterrupted time, do it and then get to work.

I consider "main projects" those that require the most time energy and effort. Main projects are best to work on during the most productive part of your day. So, start your main projects first when you get to your place of work and save your smaller projects or routine tasks for the end of the day. It's best to schedule two Power Segments when you first get to work then two more after your mid-work-day break. Always follow each Power Segment with a fifteen-minute break. Do whatever you want on this break- this is your reward…check emails, Facebook, do jumping jacks, push ups, chat with friends, eat super foods, or whatever else you desire. Taking these little breaks allows you to feel more refreshed at the end of the day, plus you can access the power of your brain while you're taking your short break and see what inspiration comes to you. Often, new ideas and insights come to me during my fifteen-minute break. When you implement this strategy, at the end of each day you will have invested six-hours of focused energy on your main projects and will have taken 60 minutes to reward yourself by doing whatever you want. What can you accomplish by starting to work in Power Segments? I think you will be amazed as to how much more efficient and productive you become.

I realize some people don't like schedules, however, I believe they are essential to being productive and successful. Ask any successful person if they have a written daily schedule and ALL will say yes, even artists and other creative types.

Please know if you follow this schedule 80% of the time you will have tremendous success.

Why 80% of the time? Because, some days when you get to work you are not going to feel like working on your main projects and let that be okay. Perhaps use that day to catch up on your smaller projects and just handle routine tasks. However, whatever you choose to do, still consider working in Power Segments. The longer you work in focused chunks of time the more productive you will be—I promise!

Lastly, a branch manager from Merrill Lynch who I knew many years ago told me about a strategy to help focus one's thoughts that I still use today. I call it the "drawer method." He told me he compartmentalizes everything in his life in drawers. These "drawers" are not physical drawers rather they are mental images. He said, as he drives to work and upon entering his office he mentally opens his "work" drawer and closes all others. Similarly when he drives home from work he mentally opens his "family" drawer and closes all others. This mental process of closing and opening drawers allows him to be completely focused and present.

I also find this technique helpful to keep my projects organized as I go about my day. Each project of mine has a drawer and I only allow one drawer open at a time. Mentally opening and closing drawers allows me to be super focused. Try this exercise and see how it works for you, I am interested in your feedback, please email me at jaden@jadensterling.com

A Living Example of True Success

I've met a lot of people during my life and a person I met recently is Frederick Montilla, a man who epitomizes true success. Frederick is a division director with Investors Group in Calgary, Alberta. Frederick is a very successful person in the financial services industry who lives by the principle that it's important to help others regardless of the size of their portfolio.

Frederick started out in life with very little money. In fact, when he was fifteen he watched as his mother and father struggled with their finances, and he noticed his mother was always on the phone with her bank talking about loans. Soon it became obvious his parents were in trouble and were going bankrupt. Eventually, the phone calls escalated to a knock on the door, and to his surprise men came into their house taking everything they could to sell in order to pay off their debts. The only things the men were not authorized to take were the beds and stove. As the men were working their way through the house, Frederick looked over at his younger brother who was six years old and was clutching to his chest his favorite Nintendo game, not wanting to hand it over. The workers showed compassion and allowed his brother to keep the game, a gesture Frederick never forgot.

After the workers left, Frederick had many unanswered questions including, "How is this possible?" and "How is it that my mother was always on the phone with the bank and this happened?" These unanswered questions motivated Frederick to figure out how the financial system works. Still quite young, though, Frederick set out to make his own way and started delivering pizzas and cleaning airplanes for a living. Frederick married young and had a family to support yet he still had a burning desire to figure out how the financial markets worked. I guess you could say his desire was on his white board always in the forefront of his mind.

One day while picking up his mother-in-law at her place of work, which was at a large mansion, Frederick followed the prompting he felt inside and asked the owner of the home how he could afford such a big house. It turned out the home's owner was Mr. Jack Rothenberg, owner of Rothenberg and Rothenberg Investments. Mr. Rothenberg told Frederick (who was twenty at the time) to start in the mutual fund sales business. Frederick asked Mr. Rothenberg, "What are the chances of me becoming successful like you?" To which Mr. Rothenberg replied, "No one has ever asked me that. I will tell you this though, people don't care what you know until they know you care."

Frederick took the advice to heart and told himself he was going to figure out everything that wealthy people did to become wealthy and share that advice with everyone, regardless of the size of their portfolio. Frederick believes "value for many," and lives his life by that tenet. When Frederick started in the business he knew in his heart and soul he was going to be successful. Frederick focused on how he could make a positive difference for others, and in his third year in business was a top producer in his industry.

Frederick defines true success as his ability to handle his clients' portfolios with utmost integrity, which helps contribute to his clients' quality of life since they don't have to worry about their investments. Frederick listens to his clients and what they desire above finances, and keeps the bigger picture in the forefront of his mind. Frederick personally defines success by asking himself and others these simple questions:

How are people going to remember you?

Are you doing the things you love doing?

Are you healthy?

He states emphatically you can't be the richest guy in the graveyard.

Frederick has four kids, and is a true family man who creates his schedule to have time with his family. Often he is the only father accompanying his kids on school field trips, which sometimes prompts the question whether he is unemployed. Being good-natured, Frederick laughs, knowing full well he has designed his life to include balance in his spiritual, personal, and professional lives. Frederick says when priorities are set, decisions are easy; his priorities are God, family, and business.

Frederick attributes much of his success to following his gut feelings and intuition and he says by putting aside his personal wants and servicing people based on what they need, the money follows. Frederick is an amazingly abundant and generous person who practices what he preaches, and I am honored to know him.

✳ SELF-ASSESSMENT

Consider the tips below and ask yourself which resonate with you, then write those in your journal and commit to them daily.

◆ Make your word your bond.

◆ Under promise and over deliver.

◆ Get out of your comfort zone and commit to one act of bravery daily.

◆ Exercise your mind, body and spirit daily.

◆ Make life-impacting decisions from a position of strength.

◆ Vote for yourself.

◆ Change what is no longer working in your life.

◆ Focus on others' needs and give of your resources daily.

◆ What you desire to have, give first.

◆ Be of service.

◆ Give and receive in equal measure.

◆ Allow your customers to guide you to your next step in business.

◆ Remain open to people's opinions and suggestions—they might lead you to your next million-dollar idea.

◆ Nourish your body, mind and spirit with healthy and alive foods.

◆ Breathe deeply and align with your passion.

Conclusion

It's been an amazing journey! I hope that you've enjoyed reading this book as much as I've enjoyed finishing it.

The power of alchemy is real. Maybe you can't convert clay into gold with your home chemistry set, but you can do something even more powerful: you can change yourself. Alchemists used one instrument, one vessel, and one fire to make gold. You have your one instrument (mind), one vessel (body), and one fire (spirit) to create anything you want in your life. You can transform your everyday, ho-hum or even depressed existence into a life that's brimming with energy and possibility. Such a power is worth even more than gold.

We've covered a lot of life-changing information. We've discovered how to go within yourself to find the tools you already possess. The most powerful tool, we've found, is your own intuition. It's the inner compass that, if you heed what it tells you, will guide you unerringly along the path that is perfect for you.

We've talked about ego and how to go beyond the blame game. You are responsible for everything that you do and every thought in your mind. Isn't that a liberating concept? Isn't it great to know that you do not have to be the slave of circumstance or external events? That your goodness and bright soul shine through regardless of the circumstances in which you find yourself?

I've revealed the importance of nourishing your body and how something as simple as a glass of pure spring water can be a catalyst for inner transformation. We've seen how gratitude and having complete thoughts can be a powerful force for good, and how the Golden Grid can help you manifest anything you desire.

Most of all, we've discovered how we are all tuned into the vibration of the universe and to the vibration of our hearts. You are capable of creating your own reality—yes, your own physical reality—by being in tune with the energy of the universe and attracting what you want with focused thought and by taking inspired action.

Ready? Now is the time to get started on your journey to success and happiness! Align yourself with positive vibrations and feel the golden glow of energy fill your soul. See the world with new eyes. Hear with new ears. Make choices with new insight. Greet each day with an open heart. Cast off the shackles of past disappointment. Devote yourself to serving others. Transform your body with pure natural super foods. Fill your lungs with fresh clean air.

Feel the joy of life!

I want to hear about your journey. Be sure to contact me at Jaden@jadensterling.com. And sign up to receive my free newsletter, which provides a tip for you to implement in your life each week as you journey toward true success. To receive the weekly free tips please go to www.thewealthquest.com and enter your name and email address on our home page.

May blessings be upon you and your loved ones.

Acknowledgments

This book was brought to life by the help of many people, angels and spirit guides, many of whom are on the physical Earth plane and for whom I am grateful. They are: Thomas Hauck, editor (Gloucester, MA) who was extraordinarily patient and kind as he organized my notes and taught me the power of brevity. Alexis Wolf, writing coach (Olympia, WA) who has a flair for the English language and who was vital in helping me communicate my message. Anna Modig, cover design (Banana Head Graphics St. Petersburg, FL) who goes the extra mile and never tires from making the numerous changes I always ask of her. Peggy McColl, marketing consultant (Quebec, Canada) who always steers me in the right direction before I get off track, thanks Peggy I appreciate your friendship!

Special thanks to other friends and mentors who have inspired me along the way, without each of you I would have stopped writing long ago. A few special people who I am grateful for are: Peter and Robin Adams thank you for the many meaningful conversations that helped me stay focused and not lose sight of my mission. Fiona Wilfley for being a great friend and sounding board when it comes to all my projects. My cousin Anne, thank you for your support and love. Aunt Pat, thank you for always loving us when we needed it most. Cindy Smith for always believing in me and helping me share my message. Doreen Virtue for your mentorship and friendship. You inspire me to become a better person each day. Kristina Walsh for being there every time I ate way too many crackers. Your advice is always spot on, thank you! Tracy Blehm for always making me laugh and helping me to not take myself too seriously.

There are many people in the spiritual community who help bring my products to market and for whom I am grateful. Special thanks to: Jennifer Mueller (Friends and Gems), Brenda Holden (All Things Beautiful), Fred Montilla (Investors Group), Lisa K. (Between Heaven & Earth), Blog Talk Radio, and Kamen Nikolov (KD studiogroup) for keeping my website up and running.

To all the amazing people in my life through the Quantum Leap program, the Possibility Coaches Chris and Jon who kept telling me "just keep writing." Frederic Leyd for your kind support and brotherly love. Jodi Chapman and Dan Teck, you are two of the greatest friends anyone could ask for. Thank you for all your help when I needed it most on this book project, I am grateful for your friendship, love and support! I love you both! Steve Harrison for teaching me how to get my ideas out and into the world. Louise Hay for showing all of us how to change the world!

A heartfelt thank you to my step-up-kids Dylan and Dana for being so patient, loving and understanding during all the hours it took for me to finish this book. To my wife Stacey, your support and love is what keeps me going each day and I am forever grateful to have someone as special as you to share this journey with.

To my guides in the spiritual realm (The One Voice), thank you for being with me and guiding me through life. You illuminate my path with clarity and guide my fingers as I type. I am grateful. To Bladen, Mom, Kimberly, Grandma, Frisco, and all other special beings in the spiritual realm, as you know I miss you and think of you often. However, I am grateful that you all are only a thought away... I love you.

To all those who I care for and didn't mention by name, your friendship and support mean the world to me, thank you.

Gratitude to YOU, the reader, for supporting my work and helping me get my message out. I am honored to serve you and look forward to hearing from each of you. Please email me at Jaden@jadensterling.com

Thanks to Source for your big love and guidance, I am truly humbled that you have taken such a liking to me.

About the Author

A leader in the New Thought field of the Law of Attraction and Manifesting, Jaden Sterling speaks internationally on topics including "How to Have a Balanced Approach: Mind, Body and Spirit for Success," "Discovering Your Destiny," and "How to Turn Your Passion into Profit."

Jaden teaches by drawing from his personal experiences that led him to the top one percent of income earners in the United States at age 26, and to develop a multi-million dollar real estate portfolio in his thirties. Jaden says, "Although I was a slow starter—I didn't speak until I was four and couldn't tell analog time until age 11—I soon became a quick learner. Early on I knew if I were going to be successful I needed an edge that most others didn't think of, which was getting information from the most trusted source I knew. This source was already inside of me—my intuition."

The author of *Manifesting Wealth & Wisdom Daily Oracle Cards*, Jaden is committed to sharing with his growing audience how to access that special place inside themselves, so that they too can experience true success and live a life of freedom. He lives in beautiful Invermere, British Columbia, with his wife

Stacey, and step-up-kids, Dylan and Dana, and their pet turtles Cruiser and Digger.

For more information about how Jaden can help you to discover your purpose and live your passion, or to invite Jaden to speak at your next event or corporate gathering please visit http://www.thewealthquest.com.

Made in the USA
Charleston, SC
16 February 2016